THE PSALMS

heartbeat of life and worship

THE
PSALMS
*heartbeat of life
and worship*

*benedict
janecko
o.s.b.*

Cover Illustration: *Donald Walpole, O.S.B.*

Library of Congress Catalog Number
86-72734
ISBN 0-87029-203-X

© 1986 St. Meinrad Archabbey
St. Meinrad, Indiana 47577

Material appearing on pages 45 through 59 has been reprinted with permission from *Keeping the Day*, edited by William Stubbs, Latrobe, Pennsylvania, 1985.

Dedicated to my parents who first taught me to pray
and to my confreres at Saint Vincent Archabbey
who have continued to pray with me.

My heart and my flesh
cry out for the living God.
Ps 84:3

PREFACE

Vatican II urged Christians to renew themselves (the Church) by a return to Sacred Scripture. Returning to Scripture always means returning to the psalms, the heart of the Bible. If we open our Bible to its center, we find the psalms there, right at the *heart* of the Scriptures. The psalms pump blood – the Semitic symbol of life – into the rest of the Old and the New Testament. They set our hearts on fire with passion and compassion. Just as our own hearts pant, murmur, leap, beat, hammer, race, and skip, so do the psalms in terms of the rest of Scripture. God has providentially placed them at the center of the Bible and our lives (Carroll Stuhlmueller). The psalms are *heart*-core literature.

Notwithstanding laudatory praises of the psalms as the heart of the Bible and our prayer life, they are attacked in some circles as being outdated, pre-Christian, even un-Christian. We are badly in need of a "heart transplant" in the life of the Church today. By becoming Semites at heart we can acquire a new lease on our prayer life.

Some members of our Christian communities think there are too many psalms in our prayer life and liturgies. Unfortunately, these persons have created a cleavage between the Old and the New Testament, have set up false dichotomies between the God and religion of the Old Testament and the God and religion of the New. They pretend that the God of Israel is a God of wrath while the God of the Christian is one of love; that the God of Israel is a God of judgment and the Christian God is one of compassion; that the Old Testament centers around law and observance while the New centers on gospel and grace. One will find all of these qualities in both the Old and New Testaments since the God of both is one and the same, allowing for some evolution on our part in understanding the mysterious nature of this God. Paradoxically, the most scandalous sheet in the Bible is the blank sheet that separates the two Testaments.

Perhaps we best appreciate the psalms, "150 steps between death and life," when they are used in occasional ways and settings. For example, try praying Psalm 1 when in a quandary; Psalm 4 before lying down to sleep; Psalm 8 when you get down on yourself or the rest of humanity; Psalm 19 when you're in a beautiful scenic spot or with a friend, lover, or spouse under a

starlit sky with a full moon; Psalm 22 when you feel forsaken and
abandoned by friends and God; Psalm 29 while watching a
storm; Psalm 32 before celebrating the sacrament of penance or
reconciliation; Psalm 88 when, lonely and frustrated, darkness
seems your only companion; Psalm 104 when you are high on life
and the beauties of creation; Psalm 150 when you are ecstatic.
Pray your experiences and experience your prayers. The psalms
contain something for everyone in every conceivable situation.
Pray them with your mind, heart, and body. Let your feelings
and emotions take over. The psalms are meant to be "enjoyed"
and "cried," not simply recited and sung. Praise the Lord at all
times as long as you have breath (life).

One marvels at the variety within the psalms. They are written
in a number of literary forms, but the two chief types are hymns
of praise and laments, both individual and communal. One also
finds pilgrim psalms, wisdom psalms, historical psalms, enthronement psalms, royal psalms, and psalms of confidence and
hope. There are songs sung in exile, songs sung in preparation for
battle, songs sung in thanksgiving. These songs envelop every
meaningful event and everyone who is alive.

As a springboard for theological wonderings and wanderings,
the psalms offer the opportunity to reflect upon biblical motifs
appearing inside and outside the psalter. I write this booklet as a
dialogue with fellow pilgrims, hoping for a mutual transformation. Scripture — and particularly the psalms — serves as a mirror
where we see ourselves and our lives reflected. No fast rules or
guidelines keep the past separate from the present. There is a constant commingling of Israel, the Church, and the contemporary
pray-er. Often the he/she of the psalmist is interchanged with the
"I" and the "we" of the contemporary pray-er and reflecter. The
common denominator is lived human experience, the human
condition. The most satisfying response to that condition comes
by way of biblical prayer — the psalms.

Variety is also a trait of the authorship of the psalms. Although
there are still some who would ascribe the entire psalter to King
David, we associate a certain anonymity with the authorship of
the psalms. It is better to say that Israel, a corporate personality, — the people of God — wrote them.

First and foremost, the psalter is a collection of songs of the
people of God; songs tell us more about a people than their laws,
customs, wars, and history. The new generation, in its countless

songs of love and of protest, sends out signals to all humanity. To get the pulse of America, one listens to its music, its songs. So it was in ancient Israel. The ideals and needs of the new breed are embodied in their joyous chants, their sorrowful dirges, and their thankful praise.

These songs are emotional utterances, not philosophical discourses. They have the power and magic to evoke and to arouse the feelings of the writer or audience, since song and poetry have the innate ability to identify with the other and with the Totally Other. The power of language, the beauty of poetry, and the natural rhythms of life join together to orchestrate a symphony of praise or a tearful lament.

This booklet tries to capture some of this variety as it reflects on the creature's relationship with God, the Totally Other. Different aspects and faces of the creature's being in the world and involvement in a life with God are mirrored here (see table of contents). Our openness to awe and wonder in nature (Ps 29), to God's acting in history (Ps 78), to God's acting within ourselves (Ps 8) are areas of revelation. The limits of the human condition, the pits (Pss 88 and 130), sin, repentance, forgiveness (Ps 51), abandonment (Ps 22), anger, hatred, and vengeance (Ps 109 and Ps 137) receive their attention. The creature's search for God (Pss 42, 43, 63, and 84), and experience as a wayfarer and pilgrim on the earth (Pss 120 to 134) are expressed. The creature as worshiper and liturgical animal who scales the hill Zion to offer sacrifice and praise (Pss 15 and 24) is depicted. The enthronement (Pss 93, 96, 97, and 99), royal (Ps 2), and messianic psalms remind the creature of personal worth and dignity as a royal person, a creature to be trusted. A fitting conclusion to the work is the beautiful hymn to creation (Ps 104) and a doxology to end all doxologies, the close of the psalter (Ps 150).

Each section concludes with a short summary "on the nature of prayer." These summaries intimate that we are changed in the process of praying. The psalms themselves illustrate this transformation process. Many of the prayers start in the pits—in the depths—near the earth and clay which symbolize our fragility, weakness, and mortality. But mysteriously, renewal takes place while we pray. With the help of divine breath, the wind and spirit of God, we are elevated from that earth and clay to a lofty place comparable to a regal throne. God raises up the creature at prayer from dust and clay to elevated throne. Prayer gives an inkling of the death/resurrection paradigm, the mark of all religions and the greatest of all transformations. Although most of the psalms begin with and are rooted in nature or history, nearly all of them eventually lead to the temple mount and steps. All prayer finds its way to the house of the Lord where the worshipers gather to compose themselves and their songs. Songs and people are one.

The New American Bible (NAB) version, which follows the Hebrew text and numbering, is featured in this work. The Hebrew numbering usually runs one psalm ahead of the Greek and Vulgate versions as shown in this comparative resume:

NAB	Greek, Vulgate
1-8	1-8
9-10	9
11-113	10-112
114-115	113
116	114-115
117-146	116-145
147	146-147
148-150	148-150

While footnotes are omitted to enable the reader to concentrate on the text, the author acknowledges with thanks the pioneering work of H. Gunkel and S. Mowinckel along with the more recent writings of R. Murphy, L. Sabourin, C. Stuhlmueller, H. Guthrie, W. Brueggemann, C. Westermann, M. Dahood, B. Zerr, P. Drijvers, S. Terrien, A. Weiser, B.W. Anderson and O. Keel. Their research and psalmic musings are easily discovered within these pages. The works of Matthew Fox, creation theologian, have also been a delightful influence (see Suggested Reading).

Closer to home I am grateful for the interest of confreres and friends who encouraged me to continue my project when I might have preferred doing other things. My initial thanks go to Father Demetrius Dumm, O.S.B., mentor and confrere. It was he who introduced me to the Scriptures and communicated a love for sacred writ in witty fashion and steered me in the direction of biblical studies. Rector John Haag, O.S.B., of Saint Vincent Seminary, another confrere, continually affirmed my writing skills and spurred me on to pursue publishers. Confrere Fred Supek, always a noble critic, and Sister Sheila Carney, R.S.M., who added a feminine touch and eye to the manuscript, proved themselves trustworthy as accurate proofreaders and consultants. They made an arduous task somewhat easier for our competent secretary, Mrs. Sue Answine. Her rapidity and accuracy in typing is matched only by the psalmist's ability to play with words and delight in parallelism.

A final note: it took some twenty-five years to write this book. As a novice in 1958-59, I was introduced to the psalms. Since that time I have been a daily pray-er, reflecter, lover, and ofttimes teacher of the psalter. The psalms have left an indelible mark on me; my hope is to leave a similar mark on the heart of each reader.

BENEDICT JANECKO, O.S.B.

CONTENTS

An invitation to praise God
psalm 117

¹Alleluia.

> Praise the LORD, all you nations;
>> glorify him, all you peoples!
> ²For steadfast is his kindness toward us,
>> and the fidelity of the LORD endures forever.

The brevity of this song should not deceive us. This hymn of praise, this doxology of all nations, is just one of many songs of praise in the psalter, the Book of Praise.

This shortest psalm contains all the elements of praise: the invitation, as well as reasons and motives. Verse one invites all peoples to praise the Lord. Gentiles are included as well as the people of Israel. The psalm is ecumenical in nature and no one is excluded. The spirit of this psalm is reminiscent of Isaiah 2 when all nations in days to come shall stream toward the mountain of the Lord, toward Zion, toward Jerusalem, the holy city and the city of peace.

> In days to come,
> The mountain of the LORD's house
>> shall be established as the highest mountain
>> and raised above the hills.
> All nations shall stream toward it;
>> many peoples shall come and say:
> "Come, let us climb the LORD's mountain,
>> to the house of the God of Jacob,
> That he may instruct us in his ways,
>> and we may walk in his paths."
> For from Zion shall go forth instruction,
>> and the word of the LORD from Jerusalem (Is 2:2-3).

The spirit of the psalm is also hopeful of future final days akin to the "peaceable kingdom," when

> . . . the wolf shall be a guest of the lamb,

> and the leopard shall lie down with the kid;
> The calf and the young lion shall browse together,
>   with a little child to guide them.
> The cow and the bear shall be neighbors,
>   together their young shall rest;
>   the lion shall eat hay like the ox.
> The baby shall play by the cobra's den,
>   and the child lay his hand on the adder's lair.
> There shall be no harm or ruin on all my holy mountain;
>   for the earth shall be filled
>   with knowledge of the LORD,
>   as water covers the sea (Is 11:6-9).

The underlying truth of these lines is not the loss or change of personality traits or characteristics of the wolf, lamb, lion, ox, and cobra, but rather the acceptance and tolerance of each other, an openness and receptivity to the differences of the other. If such is the future hope for the animal kingdom, much more is it true of the human family. Praying in an ecumenical spirit can help usher in that kingdom, since the psalms are the common prayer of Jew, Protestant, and Catholic.

Verse two of Psalm 117 gives reasons and motives for praise: God's *chesed* and *'emeth*. *Chesed*, God's loving kindness, steadfast love, and continual mercy are expressive of covenant loyalty and covenant relationship. *'Emeth*, God's fidelity, has a strong, everlasting, enduring quality about it. It is a firm "yes" (amen) on God's part to a vested interest in us, recipients of his covenantal promises.

On the Nature of Prayer
Since all are invited to join Israel's prayer, no one is excluded. It is all-embracing, ecumenical in tone.

An invitation to choose
psalm 1

¹Happy the man who follows not
    the counsel of the wicked
Nor walks in the way of sinners,
    nor sits in the company of the insolent,
²But delights in the law of the LORD
    and meditates on his law day and night.
³He is like a tree
    planted near running water,
That yields its fruit in due season,
    and whose leaves never fade.
    [Whatever he does, prospers.]

⁴Not so the wicked, not so;
    they are like chaff which the wind drives away.
⁵Therefore in judgment the wicked shall not stand,
    nor shall sinners, in the assembly of the just.
⁶For the LORD watches over the way of the just,
    but the way of the wicked vanishes.

Biblical beginnings are often sprinkled with original blessings, with beatitudes, with happiness. Examples are the Adam and Eve story (Gn 1-2), Noah after the flood (Gn 9), Abraham and Sarah (Gn 12: 1-3), Jacob (Israel) and his descendant Joseph (Ex 1), and Job (Jb 1; 1f). The psalter is no exception. It, too, commences with a beatitude, a blessing, a happy note.

This song contrasts the just or righteous person with the wicked one. Reminding us that we are a choosing people as well as a chosen people, it invites us to make a choice. Life and death are daily before us; we must choose. Destiny is in our own hands as well as in the hands of God. We are the co-creators and co-determiners of our lot and of our life.

In verse one the key to happiness is presented first in a negative fashion: the just person avoids evil company.

Verse two takes a more positive posture: the just person delights in the law of the Lord, meditating on his law day and night.

The "law" here has no legalistic tone. It encompasses much richer meanings such as Torah, instruction, revelation, Scripture, story, God's word and will for humankind. It is sound advice — a guide and norm for choosing life. It teaches us how to sit, stand, and walk in the way of the Lord. The law is a light to guide us so that we do not stumble or fall.

The just person meditates on this law day and night. In chapter three of John's Gospel, one commentator identifies Nicodemus, a Jewish leader who went to see Jesus at night, as a just man. Usually people did not make nightly visits to another's house. This suggests that Nicodemus might have stayed awake all night, meditating on the law.

Verse three compares the righteous person with a tree planted near running water, a rarity in arid Palestine. Likewise the just person is often rare, as Scripture speaks frequently of a search for a single just person.

Trees dot the forest of Scripture from Genesis through Revelation. We move from the Garden of Eden with its tree of life, the tree of death, the tree of knowledge of good and evil, the cosmic tree, to Israel the tree, to the tree of the cross, and on to Revelation where we find the trees laden with jewels. The Lord has planted and often pruned all of these so that they yield fruit in due season. The prospering tree near running water is the biblical image of spiritual health, wholeness, and holiness. It symbolizes the man or woman who "has it all together," who sees a relationship among nature, humankind, and God.

Water — living, flowing — is often a biblical symbol for life, for in arid Palestine water means "life," the difference between life and death. Edward Hays writes that scribes had the obligation to take a ritual bath in living, flowing water before they began to copy the Torah. This particular psalm witnesses to such scribal piety since it demonstrates great reverence for the law and for Scripture. It is linked to the postexilic wisdom movement where the study of Scripture becomes a means of salvation.

"Not so the wicked, not so" (verse four) contrasts the wicked with the righteous and compares the wicked with chaff which the wind drives away. The life span of the wicked is short-term, short-lived, vanishing (Pss 37 and 73). They have no roots, no depth, no stability; easily scattered, they leave no trace or enduring effect. Many psalms use rural life images. The Palestinian way of separating wheat and grain from the chaff was commonplace. This is true even today in the Middle East. The good grain settles on the ground or on the threshing floor while the chaff is blown away — vanishes. Likewise the just person has weight *(kabod)* and dignity, and is not blown about by every current fad or wind.

Verse five warns that judgment is coming. The wicked, having no future, will not be permitted to mingle with the just. They will be separated from the just in the same way as chaff is separated from the wholesome grain.

I call this psalm our "fundamental option." It challenges the Jew and Christian to choose between good and evil, to opt for life or death. Beginning with an Old Testament beatitude (happy), it offers all an invitation to become the "most happy one" who will grow and prosper just as did the tree planted near running water. It is a call to mature, adult responsibility. The mature Christian is a man or woman rooted like this tree near the stream of God's love, near the courts of the Lord, growing and prospering, despite occasional setbacks of aridity, sterility, and lackluster of soul.

The spirit of Psalm 1 is parallel to the passage in Deuteronomy (30:15f): "Here, then, I have today set before you life and prosperity, death and doom. If you obey the commandments of the Lord, your God . . . you will live. . . . Choose life, then, that you and your descendants may live, by loving the Lord, your God, heeding his voice, and holding fast to him. For that will mean life for you, a long life for you. . . ."

This psalm serves as an introduction to the psalter but it also serves as an apt opening to a life of the spirit, an animated life. Although placed first as a preface to the psalter, it is not the first to be written.

On the Nature of Prayer
Prayer is transformational, not informational. Prayer is invitatory, invitational. Prayer, like life, involves choices. Prayer will make one a most happy creature.

Other psalms that invite us to choose between good and evil, between life and death, are 37, 49, 73, 91, 112, 119, 127, 128, 133, 139; these are also known as the wisdom psalms or didactic psalms.

Awe and wonder,
the Lord of the storm
psalm 29

¹*A psalm of David.*

Give to the LORD, you sons of God,
    give to the LORD glory and praise,
²Give to the LORD the glory due his name;
    adore the LORD in holy attire.

³The voice of the LORD is over the waters,
    the God of glory thunders,
    the LORD, over vast waters.
⁴The voice of the LORD is mighty;
    the voice of the LORD is majestic.
⁵The voice of the LORD breaks the cedars,
    the LORD breaks the cedars of Lebanon.
⁶He makes Lebanon leap like a calf
    and Sirion like a young bull.
⁷The voice of the LORD strikes fiery flames;
⁸   the voice of the LORD shakes the desert,
    the LORD shakes the wilderness of Kadesh.
⁹The voice of the LORD twists the oaks
    and strips the forests,
    and in his temple all say, "Glory!"

¹⁰The LORD is enthroned above the flood;
    the LORD is enthroned as king forever.
¹¹May the LORD give strength to his people;
    may the LORD bless his people with peace!

This psalm is very likely the oldest in the psalter. It is a Yahwistic adaptation borrowed from an older Canaanite hymn to Baal, the storm god. His name often appears in Scripture and he is depicted in iconography with lightning bolt in hand. Fertility of crops and progeny are his domain, while rain and storms are his instruments for blessing or cursing.

Someone has said that all formative revelatory events — all religions in fact — are born in and out of wonder. Wonder and awe

are closely linked with the experience of the holy; both have as
their object a mystery that is at once fearful and promising. There
is no substantial difference between a wonder experience and a
holy experience. The sacred and the secular are so related that the
sacred manifests itself only in and through the profane.

This psalm is a meditation on the joy of sound, a wedding of
sound and sense (S. Terrien). It is God's version of "son et lu-
mière" (sound and light show) demonstrated in a storm. A great
portion of revelation centers around "listening" to each "now" as
Israel's chief task. Every pious Jew starts the day with the prayer
called the "Shema": *Shema, Israel, Adonai Elohenu, Adonai ehad
— Hear, O Israel, the Lord is our God, the Lord alone* (Dt 6:4).
Psalm 29 is God's invitation to listen to his power and majesty in
the storm and to praise that majestic power.

The psalmist seems to be describing a thunderstorm as it cus-
tomarily moves in from the Mediterranean (verse 3), makes the
mountains of Phoenicia (Lebanon) quake as it passes over them
(verse 5) and then moves inland over the desert to Kadesh in the
region of Mount Hermon (verse 8). The psalm is as powerful as
that lightning and thunder.

The voice of thunder is the voice of God *(qol Adonai)*, repeat-
ed seven times in the psalm like thundering theophanic tom-toms
and theo-throbs which make an impression on the ear and heart
of the listener just as lightning makes its mark on the bark of the
tree (verse 9). Such is the power and the glory of God, the lord of
nature. The fact that this storm is "natural" removes none of the
wonder. Ultimately it is God at work, revealing himself in nature. God uses the simple elements of nature to accompany his
marvels in history just as Christians employ the natural elements
of water, bread, wine, and oil in their sacraments.

The psalm goes on to show that Yahweh, not Baal, is lord of
fertility; that Yahweh, not Baal, has harnessed the waters, putting order into chaos (the biblical notion of creation); that Yahweh, not Baal, is king (verse 10). The mere transposition of the
name Yahweh for Baal has transfigured and transmogrified an
ancient Canaanite hymn to the storm god into a song that Israel
sings because the song matches Israel's own experience of the numinous (the Holy).

ON THE NATURE OF PRAYER
This song reminds us that prayer is often borrowed and is a

means to infiltrate our lives with the good, the noble, and the inspirational. The Canaanites had a sense of the numinous and the mysterious along with a reverential fear and awe for nature, especially in the force of a storm. The Israelites borrowed their expression of this experience. We, too, can borrow and learn to pray from those around us.

While a storm can fill us with both fear and awesome wonder, so do the stormy situations in our life cause us to tremble — tremble. Often trembling, quivering, shaking, are signs of an encounter with the Holy and the Wholly Other. We tremble when we are fearful and when we are fascinated, when we suffer and when we experience ecstasy. Whatever the circumstance, God's presence can help us weather the storms in our lives.

Other psalms that enkindle awe and wonder are 8, 104, 139.

God acts in history
psalm 78

¹*A maskil of Asaph.*

Hearken, my people, to my teaching;
    incline your ears to the words of my mouth.
²I will open my mouth in a parable,
    I will utter mysteries from of old.
³What we have heard and know,
    and what our fathers have declared to us,
⁴We will not hide from their sons;
    we will declare to the generation to come
The glorious deeds of the Lord and his strength
    and the wonders that he wrought.
⁵He set it up as a decree in Jacob,
    and established it as a law in Israel,
That what he commanded our fathers
    they should make known to their sons;
⁶So that the generation to come might know,
    their sons yet to be born,
That they too may rise and declare to their sons
⁷   that they should put their hope in God,
And not forget the deeds of God
    but keep his commands,
⁸And not be like their fathers,
    a generation wayward and rebellious,
A generation that kept not its heart steadfast
    nor its spirit faithful toward God.

⁹The sons of Ephraim, ordered ranks of bowmen,
    retreated in the day of battle.
¹⁰They kept not the covenant with God;
    according to his law they would not walk;
¹¹And they forgot his deeds,
    the wonders he had shown them.
¹²Before their fathers he did wondrous things,
    in the land of Egypt, in the plain of Zoan.
¹³He cleft the sea and brought them through,
    and he made the waters stand as in a mound.

¹⁴He led them with a cloud by day,
    and all night with a glow of fire.
¹⁵He cleft the rocks in the desert
    and gave them water in copious floods.
¹⁶He made streams flow from the crag
    and brought the waters forth in rivers.

¹⁷But they sinned yet more against him,
    rebelling against the Most High in the wasteland,
¹⁸And they tempted God in their hearts
    by demanding the food they craved.
¹⁹Yes, they spoke against God, saying,
    "Can God spread a table in the desert?
²⁰For when he struck the rock, waters gushed forth,
    and the streams overflowed;
  Can he also give bread
    and provide meat for his people?"
²¹Then the LORD heard and was enraged;
    and fire blazed up against Jacob,
    and anger rose against Israel,
²²Because they believed not God
    nor trusted in his help.
²³Yet he commanded the skies above
    and the doors of heaven he opened;
²⁴He rained manna upon them for food
    and gave them heavenly bread.
²⁵The bread of the mighty was eaten by men;
    even a surfeit of provisions he sent them.
²⁶He stirred up the east wind in the heavens,
    and by his power brought on the south wind.
²⁷And he rained meat upon them like dust,
    and, like the sand of the sea, winged fowl,
²⁸Which fell in the midst of their camp
    round about their tents.
²⁹So they ate and were wholly surfeited;
    he had brought them what they craved.
³⁰They had not given over their craving,
    and their food was still in their mouths,
³¹When the anger of God rose against them
    and slew their best men,
    and laid low the young men of Israel.

³²Yet for all this they sinned still more
    and believed not in his wonders.
³³Therefore he quickly ended their days and their years
    with sudden destruction.
³⁴While he slew them they sought him
    and inquired after God again,

³⁵Remembering that God was their rock
  and the Most High God, their redeemer.
³⁶But they flattered him with their mouths
  and lied to him with their tongues,
³⁷Though their hearts were not steadfast toward him,
  nor were they faithful to his covenant.
³⁸Yet he, being merciful, forgave their sin
  and destroyed them not;
 Often he turned back his anger
  and let none of his wrath be roused.
³⁹He remembered that they were flesh,
  a passing breath that returns not.
⁴⁰How often they rebelled against him in the desert
  and grieved him in the wilderness!
⁴¹Again and again they tempted God
  and provoked the Holy One of Israel.
⁴²They remembered not his hand
  nor the day he delivered them from the foe,
⁴³When he wrought his signs in Egypt
  and his marvels in the plain of Zoan,
⁴⁴And changed into blood their streams — their running
  water, so that they could not drink;
⁴⁵He sent among them flies that devoured them
  and frogs that destroyed them.
⁴⁶He gave their harvest to the caterpillar,
  the fruits of their toil to the locust.
⁴⁷He killed their vines with hail
  and their sycamores with frost.
⁴⁸He gave over to the hail their beasts
  and their flocks to the lightning.
⁴⁹He loosed against them his fierce anger,
   wrath and fury and strife,
   a detachment of messengers of doom.
⁵⁰When he measured the course of his anger
   he spared them not from death,
   and delivered their beasts to the plague.
⁵¹He smote every first-born in Egypt,
   the first fruits of manhood in the tents of Ham;
⁵²But his people he led forth like sheep
   and guided them like a herd in the desert.
⁵³He led them on secure and unafraid,
   while he covered their enemies with the sea.
⁵⁴And he brought them to his holy land,
   to the mountains his right hand had won.
⁵⁵And he drove out nations before them;
   he distributed their inheritance by lot,
   and settled the tribes of Israel in their tents.

⁵⁶But they tempted and rebelled against
　　God the Most High, and kept not his decrees.
⁵⁷They turned back and were faithless like their fathers;
　　they recoiled like a treacherous bow.
⁵⁸They angered him with their high places
　　and with their idols roused his jealousy.
⁵⁹God heard and was enraged
　　and utterly rejected Israel.
⁶⁰And he forsook the tabernacle in Shiloh,
　　the tent where he dwelt among men.
⁶¹And he surrendered his strength into captivity,
　　his glory into the hands of the foe.
⁶²He abandoned his people to the sword
　　and was enraged against his inheritance.
⁶³Fire consumed their young men,
　　and their maidens were not betrothed.
⁶⁴Their priests fell by the sword,
　　and their widows sang no dirges.

⁶⁵Then the LORD awoke, as wakes from sleep
　　a champion overcome with wine;
⁶⁶And he put his foes to flight
　　and cast them into everlasting disgrace.
⁶⁷And he rejected the tent of Joseph,
　　and the tribe of Ephraim he chose not;
⁶⁸But he chose the tribe of Judah,
　　Mount Zion which he loved.
⁶⁹And he built his shrine like heaven,
　　like the earth which he founded forever.
⁷⁰And he chose David, his servant,
　　and took him from the sheepfolds;
⁷¹From following the ewes he brought him
　　to shepherd Jacob, his people,
　　and Israel, his inheritance.
⁷²And he tended them with a sincere heart,
　　and with skillful hands he guided them.

In the foregoing Psalm 29, nature is a sign of God's presence. Now in Psalm 78 we focus on history as the arena of God's activity. Israel was the first people to be aware of and appreciate history as an epiphany — manifestation — of God. Hebrews describe themselves as a people in relation to God. This relationship takes place within life's experiences in the events of history. Israel often remembers and retells her history in story form, for a shared history/story arouses the emotions, the feelings, and the imagination of a people. To touch the heart is crucial. Chronology and facts for facts' sake are secondary.

The composers of these historical songs try to involve the present generation personally and emotionally with the past. They instill the now generation with the realization that they once were slaves in Egypt but have been rescued from that bondage; they have come up out of Egypt and are slaves no longer to anyone or anything. Such is the Passover message each year when the youngest son asks his father, "Why is this night different, Dad?" This night recalls Yahweh as Israel's Maker when God created Israel out of nothing as a product of his love. Israel's need and God's love for her make an animated, adventuresome story.

Israel's origins are marked by need, want, distress, oppression, and bondage (Ex 1:1f). She, in fact, was nothing with no existence of her own until God stepped onto the stage of history in her behalf and chose her to be his favorite child. God intervened in her history and gave her hope and a future. This creation of Israel as a people and a nation is similar to the creation story in Genesis. Exodus — a departure — is also a story of beginnings.

God reveals himself to Moses (Ex 3) when he discloses his name "Yahweh." The name connotes the person in biblical parlance. This name "Yahweh" stems from the Hebrew "to live," "to be alive." Yahweh is God of the living; he is God for us, related to us, among us. He is not some aloof supreme being or unmoved mover as the Greeks would say. He is a relational person, a moved mover, present and compassionate to his people, present to them in history, in their future: "Just watch, just wait. Your future and mine are bound up together; you are my people and I am your God." God is a "prepositional" God, a "with-ness" (M. Fox) rather than a propositional God. This close-to-Israel God comes to her rescue, liberates her, overthrows the mighty and exalts the lowly. In this sense the Exodus story and many of the psalms are revolutionary. They are hope-filled literature. There is a way out — an exodus — because God is with us.

This psalm (verses 1-8) speaks of God's fidelity and Israel's base ingratitude. It tries to teach the current generation via story; these verses stress the importance of tradition (story) and the didactic device of song. Tevye used this device when he sang "Tradition" in the musical production, *Fiddler on the Roof*. To listen, remember, and pay attention to the mighty deeds and wonders of the Lord in history — in life — are important. Do not be like your ancestors; for you, the recipients and beneficiaries of the promises, must now become the conveyers. You who have drunk the waters of life must now become the "bucket brigade" so that others may drink. All these warnings are for naught, though, since this generation too will eventually turn its back (verse 57).

In verses 9 through 39 we witness the disloyalty and disobedience of God's people, their refusal to believe in wonders while God remains faithful. It would seem that Israel's forgetfulness is matched by God's remembering, Israel's sinfulness by God's grace and favors. The mystery of God's love and the mystery of evil are still a riddle. Having no faith in God's wonders is one biblical notion of sin (verse 32).

Farther on (verses 40 to 64) the people move from the desert and wilderness to countless marvels associated with the Exodus from Egypt, their conquest of the land and the subsequent trouble from the Philistines. God abandons his people momentarily to an historical force and neighboring power, the uncircumcised Philistines. The ark, the tabernacle, the tent, all symbols of God's presence with Israel, now vanish.

But then God remembers (verses 65-72). He wakes from sleep, from a stupor, to rout the enemy. He rejects Joseph, Ephraim, the northern tribes (Israel) and chooses David, Zion, Judah. This psalm clearly stems from the southern kingdom of Judah and is a highly partisan prayer. It favors the Davidic line and dynasty. David is applauded as king, warrior, shepherd who leads his people. While Psalm 29 was polemic over the matter of nature (the god of the storm), this psalm is polemic over history, over God's choice in history of Judah over Israel, of the southern kingdom over the northern tribes. The setting of this family feud is some time after the division of the monarchy around 931 B.C.E.

ON THE NATURE OF PRAYER
This psalm demonstrates that biblical prayer with its origins in history is rooted in events, in experience. It also shows that even biblical prayer is polemic at times, for instance in the feud between Judah and Israel.

Other psalms that tell of Israel's history in poetic form are 105 and 106.

The trusted creature
psalm 8

¹*For the leader; "upon the* gittith.*" A psalm of David.*

²O LORD, our Lord,
> how glorious is your name over all the earth!
> You have exalted your majesty
> above the heavens.

³Out of the mouths of babes and sucklings
> you have fashioned praise because of your foes,
> to silence the hostile and the vengeful.

⁴When I behold your heavens, the work of your fingers,
> the moon and the stars which you set in place —

⁵What is man that you should be mindful of him;
> or the son of man that you should care for him?

⁶You have made him little less than the angels,
> and crowned him with glory and honor.

⁷You have given him rule over the works of your hands,
> putting all things under his feet:

⁸All sheep and oxen,
> yes, and the beasts of the field,

⁹The birds of the air, the fishes of the sea,
> and whatever swims the paths of the seas.

¹⁰O LORD, our Lord,
> how glorious is your name over all the earth!

We have seen nature (Ps 29) and history (Ps 78) as signs of God's presence. Now we look at an even more mysterious sign of that presence: humankind.

Psalm 78 depicts humanity as a weak, sinful, rebellious people. In contrast, this song (Ps. 8) accentuates the trusted creature, the neglected side of biblical faith (W. Brueggemann). Rooted in creation theology and manifested in wisdom literature of the Old Testament, the trusted creature motif has been neglected in church readings, lectionaries, and selections in the divine office. It is true that many of the wisdom books speak about doubt, skepticism, anger with God, disbelief, cynicism, "humanism." All of these have been considered suspect, scandalous, and foreign in orthodox circles. Yet these same books speak of the trusted creature. They are positive about the human role in continual, ongoing co-creation. This person of Old Testament "enlightenment" is often the one we encounter today in our streets, marketplaces, and sometimes in the pew.

All this witnesses to the different traditions in Scripture and in the psalms. It is realistic and squares with our own notions about the human family. At times we are capable of heroics — worthy of praise. At other times, we are unreliable and deserve a reprimand.

This wisdom tradition, this creation theology, has the creature at its center. It is anthropocentric, distinct from redemption theology which has God as its center. In the latter, fallen, fragile creatures become almost as pawns and putty in God's hands, without a thought of any contribution of their own to make to God's creation. Psalm 8, however, reminds us that we need both the creature and the creator.

The trusted creature motif begins with creation stories of the world and humankind (Gn 1-2). God is good and he has made all things good: the world, man and woman, sexuality. Creation is very good; original blessing — basic goodness — is God's plan and intent (Gn 1-2) long before original sin (Gn 3) (M. Fox). Adam is Everyone and Everyone is good in the original intention of the Creator and Maker of humanity.

Later, King David becomes the prototype of every Hebrew. In his work, *In Man We Trust*, W. Brueggemann shows how David views himself as God's trusted creature. He takes great freedom in three important, sacred aspects of life: the idea of the Holy, death, and friendship. David's eating of the sacred showbread in time of need (1 Sm 21:1-6), not grieving over the death of his first born (2 Sm 12: 16-23), and his battlefield behavior with his men who risk their lives for him (2 Sm 23: 13-17) all demonstrate David as a biblical figure who saw himself as God's trusted creature. He is a choosing person as well as a chosen one. David is associated not only with the wisdom school of thought but also with cult and worship.

In the Book of Job, God himself indulges in promoting this trusted creature motif. God makes a wager with Satan concerning the uprightness and integrity of Job. God bets on Job, his creature, whom he trusts in face of trial and temptation.

Psalm 8 tries to capture this spirit. The trusted creature is the peak of God's creation, little less than a god or an angel. This creature is noble, made in the image of God. Humanity, the product of God's imagination, teaches us much about God. Psalm 8 has a democratic flavor that makes every human a noble person, a trusted creature, God's representative and image on earth. Everyone is king, and king as understood in the biblical sense has a role of service, stewardship, guardian, nurturer, peacemaker, and harmonizer. The king puts order into chaos to make all things new.

This optimistic spirit of Psalm 8 is written after the story of the Fall (Gn 3) yet still reflects the happy, original, beatitudinal biblical stance and posture about humankind. When God becomes man in Jesus, the new Adam, all that is noted above becomes even more true, for Jesus awakens in us the summons to see ourselves as the new Adam, the new creation story, new co-creators with God because we are trusted.

The opening and closing verses (2 and 10) serve as bookends to this hymn of praise where the majesty of God is exalted: "O LORD, our Lord, how glorious is your name over all the earth!" Human praise is sandwiched between God's.

In verse 3, God evokes awe and wonder from the mouths of babes and sucklings. Often the childlike creature, with the capacity for wonder, play, awe, trust, and spontaneity, is keen to notice majesty at play in the form of creative activity.

God's creative activity (verse 4) produces the heavens, the moon and the stars. His hands and fingers have set them in place, engineered, and designed and blueprinted them. How awesome, how wonder-full, how significant.

But the peak and climax is realized in verse 5: the human person. Humans stand at the center of God's creation and at the heart and center of this psalm.

The psalmist tells us in verse 6 that this creature is little less than the angels, little less than a god, one crowned like a king with glory *(kabod)* and honor.

The next verse goes on to say that God has given this creature rule and dominion over the work of his hands, entrusting all of creation to this creature — all animals and beasts, all birds and fishes of the sea, even the sea itself.

This psalm summons us to be good stewards of the land, air, seas, and waters now threatened by pollution. It reminds us that ecology is a Christian concern. The future of the planet depends on our stewardship.

ON THE NATURE OF PRAYER

Prayer is for our benefit. Prayer is to remind humans of their dignity *(kabod)*. What we think of ourselves, our self-image, influences the way we pray. In our mysterious relationship with God we must incorporate our worth and dignity as images of God while not denying our frailty, weakness, and chaotic aspects. Prayer then resembles the biblical notion of creation: putting order into chaos, an ongoing struggle, an ongoing creation.

This is why inclusive language in worship, in the psalter, and in real life is a critical human issue. There is a close relationship between how we call upon and "name God" and how we think of ourselves in everyday life. Language, naming, and world view dovetail. "Naming God," praying, and self-image are intimately linked. "Trusted creatures" must include feminine images of God and of the human in their prayer life.

There are other psalms that feature the trusted creature, such as 104 and 139, along with many psalms of trust and confidence on the part of the individual (Pss. 3, 4, 11, 16, 23, 27, 62, 121, 131) and of the community (Pss. 115, 125, 129).

Laments, the pits
psalms 88 and 130

Israel often expresed her sorrow and suffering in the form of a lament, a dirge or wailing song. She would not settle for merely a whimper, a moan or groan. From time immemorial Israel took her complaints to her compassionate God or to her wailing wall, with both hope and expectation of being heard. Nearly every lament ends on a note of confidence and hope.

One of the most baffling and scandalous arenas of God's presence and activity is the pits, the depths. Yet this should not surprise us since one of the most frequented places of creatures is the pits. More than one third of the psalms capture this human condition.

Israel's own history begins in the pits of Egyptian bondage. It is there that Israel sings her first lament as she cries out to anyone who will listen to come to her rescue (Ex 2:23). And God stooped down and heard. Israel's group history/story is already anticipated in the individual figure of the patriarch Joseph (son of Jacob/Israel), who is thrown into a pit by his own brothers before being sold into slavery (Gn 37:24). Later, the great prophet of pathos, Jeremiah, will suffer the same lot when he's thrown into an empty cistern or pit by his brothers, friends, and household (Jer 18: 20-22). Israel's laments teach us the importance of incorporating life's sufferings, crises, traumas, sins, and chaos into one's prayer life, since biblical prayer arises out of all these human experiences.

The very structure of the lament captures this human condition, often expressed in five stages. Not all five stages, however, are present in every psalm or in this order. They include: invocation, lament, pleading, acknowledgment and confession of guilt, hope and confidence in being heard. This pattern of Israelite grief and our own common human experience was thrown into striking relief by one of my students. When he missed the lament section of my psalm course, he wrote a note of explanation. I quote it in its entirety since it serves as an illustration of lament structure in any age:

Dear Ben,
Please don't take this letter as "copping out." I am simply being honest. *(invocation)*
The past three weeks have found me personally involved at home. As you well know, the whole semester has been hectic for me, culminating in my sister's death. *(lament)*
I have had literally no time to prepare a presentation. I never was one to throw something together. Please try to understand my situation. That's all I can ask. *(plea)*
I do apologize for what appears to be a lack of effort. Believe me, this is not the case. *(confession of guilt)*
Thank you for your consideration. *(confidence and anticipation of being heard).*

                                                              G.A.

This note captures and expresses all five stages of the lament structure in the order of their appearance. Such precise parallelism seems to suggest something innate about our human way of expressing ourselves in a lamentable situation.

psalm 88

[1]*A song; a psalm of the son of Korah. For the leader; according to* Mahalath. *For singing; a maskil of* Heman the Ezrahite.

[2]O LORD, my God, by day I cry out;
        at night I clamor in your presence.
[3]Let my prayer come before you;
        incline your ear to my call for help.
[4]For my soul is surfeited with trouble
        and my life draws near to the nether world.
[5]I am numbered with those who go down into the pit;
        I am a man without strength.
[6]My couch is among the dead,
        like the slain who lie in the grave,
Whom you remember no longer
        and who are cut off from your care.
[7]You have plunged me into the bottom of the pit,
        into the dark abyss.
[8]Upon me your wrath lies heavy,
        and with all your billows you overwhelm me.

⁹You have taken my friends away from me;
  you have made me an abomination to them;
  I am imprisoned, and I cannot escape.

¹⁰My eyes have grown dim through affliction;
  daily I call upon you, O LORD;
  to you I stretch out my hands.
¹¹Will you work wonders for the dead?
  Will the shades arise to give you thanks?
¹²Do they declare your kindness in the grave,
  your faithfulness among those
  who have perished?
¹³Are your wonders made known in the darkness,
  oryour justice in the land of oblivion?

¹⁴But I, O LORD, cry out to you;
  with my morning prayer I wait upon you.
¹⁵Why, O LORD, do you reject me;
  why hide from me your face?
¹⁶I am afflicted and in agony from my youth;
  I am dazed with the burden of your dread.
¹⁷Your furies have swept over me;
  your terrors have cut me off.
¹⁸They encompass me like water all the day;
  on all sides they close in upon me.
¹⁹Companion and neighbor
  you have taken away from me;
  my only friend is darkness.

Nearly every one of Israel's laments ends on a note of confidence and hope, but this psalm may be an exception to that rule. The person suffering from affliction seems close to death and the grave. The author has a rich necrological vocabulary. Terms like nether world, the pit, the dead, the grave, dark abyss, shades, darkness, and land of oblivion surface and bring many verses of this psalm as well as one's life to a close.

Much of Scripture is shrouded with salvific events occurring at night. In the first creation story, "darkness covered the abyss" (Gn 1: 2) before God steps in and says, "Let there be light" (Gn 1: 3). When God cuts a covenant with Abram (Gn 15), a deep and terrifying darkness envelops Abram — God manifests himself as a flaming torch and covenant partner only after it has become dark. The Exodus from Egypt is said to have taken place at night. Likewise, the Incarnation, too, occurred under the cover of night as the word leapt down from heaven when all was quiet, still and dark (Wis 18: 14f). Darkness even surrounds the Crucifixion; the evangelists note that it was dark from "twelve to three." Albeit symbolic, this darkness is significant. Salvific events often occur at night. Not even the Resurrection is exempt from this pattern, for the Gospels tell us that Jesus was resurrected before dawn, while it was still dark. Our God is nocturnal, our God is a night owl.

All of this suggests that God likes to dim the lights for salvific atmosphere. He loses his inhibitions and becomes creative/salvific, more spontaneous, more of a lover, his true and relational self under the cover of darkness. "For you darkness itself is not dark, and night shines as the day. [Darkness and light are the same]" (Ps 139: 12).

In his book, *The Dark Center*, E. Baltazar reminds us that darkness is the source of life and energy at all levels of being. It is the dark soil that produces crops and the dark center of the sun that is the source of light energy. Mystics have always spoken of the "dark night of the soul." Faith tells us that God can be a shadowy figure, and our response often requires that we walk in that Darkness, in his shadow.

The psalmist, in verses 2 to 9, expresses the apparent abandonment of God and the feeling of being alone in the world, alone before God—a terrifying, fascinating experience. Yet these moments of being alone are also times of opportunity and growth. They remind us that several great religions grew out of their founders' encounter with aloneness, darkness, and God: Buddha's enlightenment under the *bo* tree; Jesus' transition to new life via the tree of the cross, and Mohammed's lonely sojourn in the treeless desert.

Verses 10 to 13 remind God that he, himself, will be a loser if the psalmist is permitted to perish, for in the grave there is no praise of God (Ps 6: 6). God's PR is at stake; he has a vested interest in his creation and in his trusted creature; his honor, as well as the life of the psalmist, is on display. God has more to lose than the pray-er since he created all of life—and death.

One looks helplessly and hopelessly for some signs of confidence in this song. Besides saying the psalmist is praying (verses 2-3) these verses (10-13) in their rhetorical questioning seem to inkle, that there just might be some life beyond the grave, just maybe.

These outbursts of "hope" (verses 14-19) swiftly change into more realistic talk about misery and morbidity with the only friend left as darkness itself. Most laments end on a note of hope and confidence; this one is different since it ends with darkness. Is there not something positive about darkness?

ON THE NATURE OF PRAYER
Psalm 88 is a great psalm for middle-aged people. Dante knew this when he wrote, "In the middle of my life I find myself in a dark wood." It is also a comforting psalm for those with terminal illness.

A page from H. Nouwen's *Reaching Out* attracted my attention when I was working with this psalm:

> The roots of loneliness are very deep and cannot be touched by optimistic advertisement, substitute love images, or social togetherness. They find their food in the suspicion that there is no one who cares and offers love without conditions, and no place where we can be vulnerable without being used. The many small rejections of every day — a sarcastic smile, a flippant remark, a brisk denial or a bitter silence — may all be quite innocent and hardly worth our attention if they did not constantly arouse our basic human fear of being left totally alone with darkness as our only companion.

"The pits" is often the starting point of prayer and at times the end point as well. The only way to go out from "the pits" is up.

psalm 130

¹*A song of ascents.*

Out of the depths I cry to you, O LORD;
    Lord, hear my voice!
²Let your ears be attentive
    to my voice in supplication:

³If you, O LORD, mark iniquities,
    Lord, who can stand?
⁴But with you is forgiveness,
    that you may be revered.

⁵I trust in the LORD;
    my soul trusts in his word.
⁶My soul waits for the LORD
    more than sentinels wait for the dawn.

More than sentinels wait for the dawn,
7   let Israel wait for the Lord,
       for with the Lord is kindness
       and with him is plenteous redemption;
8And he will redeem Israel
       from all their iniquities.

One of the seven penitential psalms, the "De Profundis," is an old liturgical favorite. It continues "the pits" motif of Psalm 88. There is only one way out of "the pits," out of our own imprisonment, and that way is up (verse 1). The psalmist cries out with a loud voice to the Lord — he shouts — asking that the Lord's ears be attentive (verse 2). Sometimes Scripture gives the impression that God may have lost his hearing. The prayers of the individual and the community seem to be out of his range of hearing. This is bad news for the human ear since it is regarded as the organ of salvation. Let those who have ears (divine or human) hear.

No one is righteous before God; all are guilty. Fortunately for us God does not keep score of our faults; he is merciful forgiveness personified (verses 3-4).

He is worthy of trust and reliance (verse 5). I learn to trust my Creator who has trusted me as his creature (Ps 8). His word is forgiving, not accusatory.

So I wait for the Lord, hope in the Lord. I am confident just as a sentinel is confident as he waits for the dawn — a sure thing — although at times the wait seems long. There is light at the end of the tunnel and "the pits." Chaos and darkness give way to the light and the dawn. The Hebrew word for "wait" and "hope" is related to the one that describes "to be pregnant" and "to be in waiting," to give birth. A pregnant woman is hopeful. She anticipates the emergence of new life. She cannot yet see the fruit of her long labor but she continues to believe in the future which is within her. This psalm, "Out of the Depths," turns into a psalm of confidence and trust with a tone of Advent. Since God makes trusted creatures, then trust must be one of his hallmarks (verses 6-7).

On the Nature of Prayer
Prayer often emanates and rises "out of the depths" similar to the underground source of water (life) mentioned in the creation story (Gn 2:6) which triggers a new creation. That water becomes a life-giving source. The deeper the well, the better the water and

the prayer. It is fitting that this psalm is considered one of the "psalms of ascent" as well as a penitential psalm.

Countless other psalms of lament cry out from the depths and pits such as those of the individual: 5, 6, 7, 13, 17, 22, 25, 26, 28, 31, 35, 36, 38, 39, 42/43, 51, 54, 55, 56, 57, 59, 61, 63, 64, 69, 70, 71, 86, 88, 102, 109, 120, 130, 140, 141, 142, 143; and those of the community: 12, 44, 58, 60, 74, 77, 79, 80, 82, 83, 85, 90, 94, 106, 108, 123, 126, 137.

Repentant creature, forgiving creator psalm 51

¹*For the leader. A psalm of David,*
²*when Nathan the prophet came to him after his sin*
  with Bathsheba.

³Have mercy on me, O God, in your goodness;
    in the greatness of your compassion
    wipe out my offense.
⁴Thoroughly wash me from my guilt
    and of my sin cleanse me.

⁵For I acknowledge my offense,
    and my sin is before me always:
⁶"Against you only have I sinned,
    and done what is evil in your sight"—
That you may be justified in your sentence,
    vindicated when you condemn.
⁷Indeed, in guilt was I born,
    and in sin my mother conceived me;
⁸Behold, you are pleased with sincerity of heart,
    and in my inmost being you teach me wisdom.

⁹Cleanse me of sin with hyssop, that I may be purified;
    wash me, and I shall be whiter than snow.
¹⁰Let me hear the sounds of joy and gladness;
    the bones you have crushed shall rejoice.
¹¹Turn away your face from my sins,
    and blot out all my guilt.

¹²A clean heart create for me, O God,
    and a steadfast spirit renew within me.
¹³Cast me not out from your presence,
    and your holy spirit take not from me.
¹⁴Give me back the joy of your salvation,
    and a willing spirit sustain in me.

¹⁵I will teach transgressors your ways,
    and sinners shall return to you.

[16]Free me from blood guilt, O God, my saving God;
      then my tongue shall revel in your justice.
[17]O Lord, open my lips,
      and my mouth shall proclaim your praise.
[18]For you are not pleased with sacrifices;
      should I offer a holocaust, you would not accept it.
[19]My sacrifice, O God, is a contrite spirit;
      a heart contrite and humbled, O God,
      you will not spurn.

[20]Be bountiful, O Lord, to Zion in your kindness
      by rebuilding the walls of Jerusalem;
[21]Then shall you be pleased with due sacrifices,
      burnt offerings and holocausts;
      then shall they offer up bullocks on your altar.

This psalm, the "Miserere," is another penitential psalm, or prayer of repentance. Some may find this psalm somber in tone, but the psalmist realized that human sinfulness and God's mercy are complementary partners on the road to salvation.

Traditionally, the psalm has been attributed to David who committed adultery with Bathsheba, then murdered her husband, Uriah, to cover up his sin. David's story is told in more detail in chapters 11 and 12 of the Second Book of Samuel. The king who is often lawgiver, lawmaker, and law enforcer in the Old Testament is here depicted as lawbreaker. We are like that king since we are free to keep God's laws or break them.

The pray-er (verse 3f) asks for God's mercy and compassion to wipe out his sin. The Hebrew word for "compassion" or "tender mercy" stems from the root for "womb" *(rechem)*. Compassion which stems from the womb is God's motherlike nurturing quality that can identify with suffering and even empathize with sin. It is also linked with birthing, bringing forth new life. God does not want the death of a sinner but rather the life of a converted, newborn person. Change, transformation, and new life are the desired end product of God's forgiveness.

But first the sinner must admit and acknowledge sin, own his faults, faults that are offensive to God as well as to others (verses 5-8). Sin has the built-in capacity to bind, immobilize, paralyze, imprison a person. The only way out is grace which opens and releases us. The psalm posits the universality of sin more than it attempts to teach the doctrine of Original Sin. Sin has roots deep in human nature.

Here (verses 9-14) the psalmist turns to restoration and renewal, new creation language and images. The writer seeks repentance, not out of fear nor to acquire eternal fire insurance, but with a sincerity of heart which recognizes that a ruptured relationship exists with a significant Other. The issue is the premium on God's love insurance policy — not hell and damnation.

In return for a clean heart and renewed spirit (verses 15-19) the psalmist promises to be God's PR person. He will publicize God's graciousness and generosity to sinners, for God really wants a contrite heart more than sacrifice.

Renewed individuals result in the restoration of Jerusalem (verse 20). Just as the walls of Jerusalem are rebuilt, so also shall be the shattered and tattered nature of sinners. Healing and forgiveness bind up personal wounds in the same way that mortar fills cracks in city walls.

ON THE NATURE OF PRAYER

Although the bad news declares that we are sinners, the good news shouts out that God loves sinners. We must use even sin as a means for personal growth and development. We must incorporate all the ambiguities of life into our adult Christian life and spirituality. Our attitudes toward sin are important. We can go through life believing with Judas that our sin is too great; it cannot be forgiven. Or we can take Peter's stance who, on the day of his "first communion and ordination," wept bitterly over his sin of Christ's betrayal. But he did not despair. The notion of "being a David" and understanding ourselves as trusted creatures extends even into the mysterious realms of sin. Like David we must put our sins behind us and get on with life; we must take our handicaps and use them as instruments for growth in health, wholeness, and holiness, for the mystery of God and the mystery of sin are interwoven. With this attitude, God will "cover up" for us and blot out our sins.

This psalm is a good preparation for the sacrament of reconciliation. It has the traditional ingredients for celebrating this sacrament: an examination of conscience; an attitude of sorrow; firm purpose of amendment; admission and confession of sins; and finally, a promise to do penance and to turn one's life around.

In addition to Psalm 51, a psalm protesting innocence such as Psalm 69 might be included here.

Abandoned creature
psalm 22

¹*For the leader; according to "The hind of the dawn."*
A psalm of David.

²My God, my God, why have you forsaken me,
    far from my prayer,
    from the words of my cry?
³O my God, I cry out by day, and you answer not;
    by night, and there is no relief for me.
⁴Yet you are enthroned in the holy place,
    O glory of Israel!
⁵In you our fathers trusted;
    they trusted, and you delivered them.
⁶To you they cried, and they escaped;
    in you they trusted,
    and they were not put to shame.
⁷But I am a worm, not a man;
    the scorn of men, despised by the people.
⁸All who see me scoff at me;
    they mock me with parted lips,
    they wag their heads:
⁹"He relied on the Lord; let him deliver him,
    let him rescue him, if he loves him."
¹⁰You have been my guide since I was first formed,
    my security at my mother's breast.
¹¹To you I was committed at birth,
    from my mother's womb you are my God.
¹²Be not far from me, for I am in distress;
    be near, for I have no one to help me.

¹³Many bullocks surround me;
    the strong bulls of Bashan encircle me.
¹⁴They open their mouths against me
    like ravening and roaring lions.
¹⁵I am like water poured out;
    all my bones are racked.
My heart has become like wax
    melting away within my bosom.

¹⁶My throat is dried up like baked clay,
    my tongue cleaves to my jaws;
    to the dust of death you have brought me down.
¹⁷Indeed, many dogs surround me,
    a pack of evildoers closes in upon me;
  They have pierced my hands and my feet;
¹⁸   I can count all my bones.
  They look on and gloat over me;
¹⁹   they divide my garments among them,
    and for my vesture they cast lots.

²⁰But you, O Lord, be not far from me;
    O my help, hasten to aid me.
²¹Rescue my soul from the sword,
    my loneliness from the grip of the dog.
²²Save me from the lion's mouth;
    from the horns of the wild bulls, my wretched life.

²³I will proclam your name to my brethren;
    in the midst of the assembly I will praise you:
²⁴"You who fear the Lord, praise him;
    all you descendants of Jacob, give glory to him;
    revere him, all you descendants of Israel!
²⁵For he has not spurned nor disdained
    the wretched man in his misery,
  Nor did he turn his face away from him,
    but when he .cried out to him, he heard him."
²⁶So by your gift will I utter praise in the vast assembly;
    I will fulfill my vows before those who fear him.
²⁷The lowly shall eat their fill;
    they who seek the Lord shall praise him:
    "May your hearts be ever merry!"

²⁸All the ends of the earth
    shall remember and turn to the Lord;
  All the families of the nations
    shall bow down before him.
²⁹For dominion is the Lord's,
    and he rules the nations.
³⁰To him alone shall bow down
    all who sleep in the earth;
  Before him shall bend
    all who go down into the dust.
  And to him my soul shall live;
³¹   my descendants shall serve him.
  Let the coming generation be told of the Lord
³²   that they may proclaim to a people
    yet to be born
    the justice he has shown.

"My God, my God, why have you forsaken me?" One cannot begin reading this psalm without thinking of Jesus' crucifixion and death. The enemies' scorn and derision, the vinegar to quench the thirsting Jesus, the pierced hands and feet, the lots cast for his garments, all remind the Christian of Calvary. Before climbing Calvary, we might want to steep ourselves in the human condition for an understanding of this psalm. It speaks on its own merits first and foremost as a remarkable model and paradigm of the human condition both before and after Christ. It characterizes the structure of laments in that verses 2 to 22 make known the cry, the lament, and the plea for help, while the end of the psalm (verses 23-32) concludes on a note of confidence as do most laments. The very literary structure, then, lends itself to a passion/death/resurrection model. Our own life/death/new life experience is at stake. The experience of our faith in God is equally being tried and tested.

The psalmist cries out to God (verse 2) but he seems so far away, so distant. Why are you so far away, God? Are you deaf? losing your hearing? aloof? apathetic?

Day and night the psalmist cries out (verse 3), but he gets no answer. "Address unknown" and "unlisted number" must pass through the psalmist's mind. There is no relief in sight. The spiritual Rolaid era has not yet dawned.

Remembering helps. Our ancestors in the faith called upon you, trusted in you, and they found relief and deliverance (verse 5). But where are you when *I* need you? You heed not my plea. I feel like a worm and no man (verse 7f). What has happened to the lofty image — the person made in the image of God, the trusted creature, one little less than a god or an angel (Ps 8)? People walk over me and crush me like a worm without even realizing they are stomping upon me. They scorn, mock, scoff, deride.

Rumor has it that this person trusted in God (verse 9); then let God deliver him. Let angels come to his rescue. Shouldn't angels rush to rescue their peer — a human — who is little less than a god?

Fleeting moments of confidence surface (verse 10ff). From my birth and even while still in the womb, I was dedicated to you, committed to you, felt secure in your presence as at my mother's breast. Why do you abort me now, oh God? You were so close to me once. Now you seem so far away, so distant.

Verses 13 to 22 speak of raging bulls, roaring lions, and wild dogs, all symbols of the psalmist's enemies and persecutors.

Chaos and death unleash themselves against the psalmist. His enemies and ours (our doubts?) surround us and close in on us. The demonic forces of bulls, lions, and dogs of our lives gnaw away at us, gore us, tear us and rip us apart in a slow, painful way. They resemble a lion playing with his prey, resemble physical and cognitive crucifixion. We feel threatened, afraid. And we tremble. Are we perhaps in the presence of the Holy? Or is it the Evil One? When did you last tremble and shake? Maybe we are in the presence of the Holy. Maybe.

The psalmist feels weak and dry, dehydrated, lacking water of the spirit; it is the "dry night of the soul" (verse 15f). He is like water poured out. He is consumed much like the hot fiery desert sands gulp down water. His throat is dried up like baked clay while his tongue cleaves to his jaws. "How dry I am" is more than a drinking song to this person who feels dried up, sterile, unproductive, soaked up by uncontrollable situations.

Be not far from me, O Lord; come to my rescue (verses 20-22). Although the faith of others can be a pillar of support to me, my faith must not become parasitic; I must make my faith personal, make it my own. I must learn to recognize God's power, his action in my life.

At this point (verses 23-32), the psalm takes a sudden twist. It changes from a lament to a prayer of hope, one of confidence and praise. Something has happened to the pray-er. In the course of praying, one's outlook has changed. Speculation has it that a cultic official, priest, or prophet assured the pray-er in a visit to the temple or shrine that one's situation would improve. The rest of the psalm witnesses to the psalmist's trust and confidence in hearing God's saving word through a cultic minister. God does hear the cries of those in misery (verse 25). The psalmist wants to be a witness of God's saving action to others; he wants to share the Good News.

His spreading of the Gospel will not be limited to the local area (verses 28-32). These verses have a universal ring that echoes to the ends of the earth, extending the good news to the living and the dead as well as to all those yet unborn. All shall hear of God's justice. The "now" generation of faith is the link between past and future believers.

On the Nature of Prayer

In Psalm 22, we have seen the psalmist move from sadness to

gladness, from lament to praise and hope, from abandonment to acceptance. This change seemed to occur gradually while the person was in the act of praying. Transformation appears to be an inherent quality of prayer.

A Christian cannot sidestep the cross. As we try to incorporate creative suffering into our Christian life-style, we must often resort to reckless abandon — total trust — while we deal with what appears to be divine abandonment. The Gospels of Matthew (27:46) and John (19:23ff) put this psalm on the lips of Jesus at the time of his Passion. The psalm graphically describes Jesus' plight when he is stripped not only of his garments, but also of his dignity; when he seems more a worm than a man; when he is naked and vulnerable. Jesus prays this psalm in its entirety on the cross. His very life and prayer become one at that moment when he passes from death to life. This psalm, which has the power to change our tears into dancing (Ps 30: 11), transforms Jesus while he prays.

In addition to Psalm 22, some verses of Psalms 44 and 80 address the abandoned creature.

Creature capable
of hatred and vengeance
psalms 109 and 137

psalm 109

¹*For the leader. A psalm of David.*

O God, whom I praise, be not silent,
2   for they have opened wicked and
     treacherous mouths against me.
They have spoken to me with lying tongues,
3   and with words of hatred
     they have encompassed me
     and attacked me without cause.
⁴In return for my love they slandered me,
     but I prayed.
⁵They repaid me evil for good
     and hatred for my love.

⁶Raise up a wicked man against him,
     and let the accuser stand at his right hand.
⁷When he is judged, let him go forth condemned,
     and may his plea be in vain.
⁸May his days be few;
     may another take his office.
⁹May his children be fatherless,
     and his wife a widow.
¹⁰May his children be roaming vagrants and beggars;
     may they be cast out of the ruins of their homes.
¹¹May the usurer ensnare all his belongings,
     and strangers plunder the fruit of his labors.
¹²May there be no one to do him a kindness,
     nor anyone to pity his orphans.
¹³May his posterity meet with destruction;
     in the next generation may their name
     be blotted out.
¹⁴May the guilt of his fathers be remembered by the Lord;
     let not his mother's sin be blotted out;
¹⁵May they be continually before the LORD,
     till he banish the memory of these parents
     from the earth,

16Because he remembered not to show kindness,
>but persecuted the wretched and poor and the
>brokenhearted, to do them to death.

17He loved cursing; may it come upon him;
>he took no delight in blessing; may it
>be far from him.

18And may he be clothed with cursing as with a robe;
>may it penetrate into his entrails like water
>and like oil into his bones;

19May it be for him like a garment which covers him,
>like a girdle which is always about him.

20May this be the recompense from the LORD upon my
>accusers and upon those who speak evil against me.

21But do you, O GOD, my Lord,
>deal kindly with me for your name's sake;
>in your generous kindness rescue me;

22For I am wretched and poor,
>and my heart is pierced within me.

23Like a lengthening shadow I pass away;
>I am swept away like the locust.

24My knees totter from my fasting,
>and my flesh is wasted of its substance.

25And I am become a mockery to them;
>when they see me, they shake their heads.

26Help me, O LORD, my God;
>save me, in your kindness,

27And let them know that this is your hand;
>that you, O LORD, have done this.

28Let them curse, but do you bless;
>may my adversaries be put to shame,
>but let your servant rejoice.

29Let my accusers be clothed with disgrace
>and let them wear their shame like a mantle.

30I will speak my thanks earnestly to the LORD,
>and in the midst of the throng I will praise him,

31For he stood at the right hand of the poor man,
>to save him from those who would condemn him.

psalm 137

1By the streams of Babylon we sat and wept
>when we remembered Zion.

2On the aspens of that land
>we hung up our harps,

3Though there our captors asked of us
>the lyrics of our songs,
>and our despoilers urged us to be joyous:
>"Sing for us the songs of Zion!"

4How could we sing a song of the LORD
    in a foreign land?
5If I forget you, Jerusalem,
    may my right hand be forgotten!
6May my tongue cleave to my palate
    if I remember you not,
    if I place not Jerusalem ahead of my joy.

7Remember, O LORD, against the children of Edom,
    the day of Jerusalem, when they said,
    "Raze it, raze it down to its foundations!"
8O daughter of Babylon, you destroyer,
    happy the man who shall repay you
    the evil you have done us!
9Happy the man who shall seize and smash
    your little ones against the rock!

Most people can handle glad songs and sad ones but few can deal in a meaningful, positive way with "mad" songs found in the psalter. In this grouping of psalms (maledictory and cursing), censorship of Scripture has been historically most evident. How can the Christian pray these psalms that deal with destroying one's enemies and smashing Babylonian babies' heads against a rock?

It is important to remember that the psalms are emotional utterances, emotional shouts. Feelings predominate; feelings run the gamut of all human experience. The ability to express anger as well as love makes us human and keeps us human. The psalms permit and help us do this. Both anger and love energize us to get the adrenalin flowing.

The Bible is teeming and seething with furious figures. Angry, protesting, prophetic people often go hand in hand. The prophet Amos, a simple, lowly shepherd, was forced to "moonlight" as a dresser of sycamore trees. Only in this way could he eke out a living at a time when the distinction between rich and poor was mounting in Judah and Israel. As a hard working shepherd, he tenderly cared for his flock which would eventually end up on the banquet tables of the rich without much recompense to Amos for his arduous labors. Tired of this corruption, inequity, and rip-off by the rich, Amos decides to do something about it. He does so in an angry, hateful way and with a vengeance. Anger and rage, then, can be prayerful as well as therapeutic when we address God in this fashion about significant concerns.

The prophet Jeremiah is another prophetic voice who rages with anger and curses his horrendous and treacherous situation in his so-called *Confessions.* In his anger, he curses the wicked because they prosper and his family who plots against him. He curses the day he was born and calls God a treacherous brook, withholding his promised help and duping him. Prayers for vengeance against his enemies and against God are sprinkled throughout his prayer life.

The patient Job of the *Prologue* turns into an impatient, cursing, angry figure in the *First Cycle of Speeches (Dialogues)* as he ponders the reasons for his suffering when he is a just and innocent man.

Psalms 109 and 137 are written in this same spirit. The psalmist asks for vengeance but he leaves that vengeance in the hands of God. He is being honest with his feelings. All of us at one time or another want revenge, retaliation, vengeance. We want wrongs set straight, we want to be proven right. These two psalms capture our inner feelings. When we've been hurt, betrayed, defeated, we want to even the score.

The language of these psalms is hyperbolic. Linguistically, overkill is at work. The litany of curses (Ps 109:6-19) manifests a creative variety differing from our own oft-repeated four-letter words which reflect our limited cursing vocabulary. In this litany a variety of curses is leveled at the enemy: may his life be shortened; his father's life end; his children orphaned and his wife widowed; may someone take his belongings and his name die out to fade into oblivion. These harsh slurs and curses teach a lofty biblical belief in a roundabout way; even these curses placed upon his family and others suggest the importance of corporate personality. Both blessings and curses fall upon the entire community suggesting that our destinies are somehow locked and linked together. They highlight the communal, social, and public nature of the biblical message. Since these curses are aimed at the family, tribe, or clan, the individual becomes less important than the social and familial unit. A togetherness is involved whether that be for salvation or damnation, for blessing or for curse. We are saved or lost as "family" (as church), not as individuals, a dimension that we moderns have lost sight of. The corporate personality concept often found in the Hebrew Scriptures is akin to the Mystical Body of Christ concept. It challenges contemporary Christians to rethink their understanding of salvation and damnation, an understanding often based on rugged individualism and a "Jesus and me" spirituality. Moreover, it urges Christians to take into account the social, communal, public nature of revelation, of religious thinking and acting. Psalm 109 stresses the community aspect of life, prayer, cursing, and blessing.

The curses uttered here cover all aspects of time: past, present, and future, and no one is spared—even future generations. The curses are far-reaching, thorough, all-inclusive, with a power comparable to blessing. Once spoken, they have an existence that only God in his mercy and compassion can alter.

The biblical curse is also related to the biblical theory of retribution. At the time when the psalms were composed there was no existing firm belief in the afterlife. The ancients sought justice here and now with immediate retaliation and recompense. The "hate the sin, love the sinner" concept of later theology had not yet developed. Evil seemed bigger than life and had to be fought here and now, for if not here, then where? *Now* is the acceptable time for blessing and for curse, for choosing life or death.

Psalm 137 is another psalm that the liturgical assembly often omits or censors. It recalls the time of the Babylonian exile with all its hardships and trials, when it was difficult or impossible to sing the songs of Zion, when the mere thought and remembrance of Jerusalem was heartrending and heartbreaking. In 586 B.C.E. the Babylonians invaded Judah and the city Jerusalem. They razed the city, destroyed the temple, deported many of its peoples, and helped eclipse belief in God. "God is dead" theology started in this period.

Eventually the tables were turned. The survivors returned to their native land, but they did not forget their captors—the Babylonians. They wanted retribution and to see justice done. In this context of past harsh treatment—even death—they sought revenge, retaliation, and vengeance in prayer form. They chose a community forum, where pent-up anger and rage could be vented in assembly, so that each one's grief could take on a "formfulness" and purpose (W. Brueggemann).

Babylon, then, becomes symbolic of the enemy and chaos, of evil and sin, of whoredom, of death. The psalmist pleads that the children of this mother—this bitch, this destroyer—be wiped off the surface of the earth. The "little ones" may not refer to infants; it is probable that the reference is to the adult population in the same way that we refer to Americans as belonging to "Uncle Sam." The constant and violent wars in the Middle East that we see through today's news media capture some of this biblical rage, anger. Pent-up feelings of hatred permeate these ancient psalms as well as the veins of contemporary Middle East people. They seem to be on fire for good or for evil, impassioned with life in its entirety.

How can Christians pray these psalms? Despite the foregoing rationale, many Christians still have problems with these songs since the message that Jesus taught is love of neighbor, even love of enemies. Why then, many Christians ask, do we continue to mouth these pre-Christian and sub-Christian prayers?

These same Christians, however, may like to bomb the adult bookstore, endorse capital punishment, care little about racism or sexism, justice and peace, the evils of nuclear armament, human rights, or a cure for AIDS. Such Christians were silent during the Jewish Holocaust that the modern "Babylonian," Hitler, carried out. They were silent during the bombing of Hiroshima and Nagasaki, during the race riots of the sixties, during the prison riots of Attica, during the Vietnam War.

In truth, all of us still carry pre-Christian and sub-Christian traits within us. Christ is still on the horizon more than he is a sure solid possession. When we acknowledge this, we will be able to pray these "cursing" psalms with gusto and fervor.

ON THE NATURE OF PRAYER

"Cursing" psalms still serve a purpose. When addressed to God, anger and rage about significant concerns are both prayerful and therapeutic. A concern for justice and peace can be the outcome.

Psalms 58, 69, and 82 are in a spirit akin to Psalms 109 and 137 treated above.

Creature as God searcher
psalms 42, 43, 63, 84

psalm 42

¹*For the leader. A* maskil *of the sons of Korah.*

²As the hind longs for the running waters,
  so my soul longs for you, O God.
³Athirst is my soul for God, the living God.
  When shall I go and behold the face of God?
⁴My tears are my food day and night,
  as they say to me day after day,
  "Where is your God?"
⁵Those times I recall,
  now that I pour out my soul within me,
When I went with the throng
  and led them in procession to the house of God,
Amid loud cries of joy and thanksgiving,
  with the multitude keeping festival.
⁶ Why are you so downcast, O my soul?
  Why do you sigh within me?
  Hope in God! For I shall again be thanking him,
  in the presence of my savior and my God.

⁷Within me my soul is downcast;
  so will I remember you
From the land of the Jordan and of Hermon,
  from Mount Mizar.
⁸Deep calls unto deep in the roar of your cataracts;
  All your breakers and your billows pass over me.
⁹By day the LORD bestows his grace,
  and at night I have his song,
  a prayer to my living God.
¹⁰I sing to God, my rock:
  "Why do you forget me?
Why must I go about in mourning,
  with the enemy oppressing me?"
¹¹It crushes my bones that my foes mock me,
  as they say to me day after day,
  "Where is your God?"

12   Why are you so downcast, O my soul?
        Why do you sigh within me?
        Hope in God! For I shall again be thanking him,
        in the presence of my savior and my God.

psalm 43

¹Do me justice, O God, and fight my fight
    against a faithless people;
    from the deceitful and impious man rescue me.
²For you, O God, are my strength.
    Why do you keep me so far away?
Why must I go about in mourning,
    with the enemy oppressing me?
³Send forth your light and your fidelity;
    they shall lead me on and bring me
    to your holy mountain, to your dwelling-place.
⁴Then will I go in to the altar of God,
    the God of my gladness and joy;
Then will I give you thanks upon the harp,
    O God, my God!
⁵Why are you so downcast, O my soul?
    Why do you sigh within me?
    Hope in God! For I shall again be thanking him,
    in the presence of my savior and my God.

In his Rule, St. Benedict has the novice master frequently ask the novice if he truly seeks God, since all good things begin with desire. It is the way to the Holy.

This group of four psalms displays an intense desire and a longing for God and his house — the temple. A craving: "As the hind longs for the running waters, so my soul longs for you, O God" (Ps 42:2), and ". . . for you my flesh pines and my soul thirsts like the earth, parched, lifeless and without water" (Ps 63:2) are apt images to describe this longing.

In Psalm 42, verses 2-6, one hears an individual lament from a person separated, banished, or in exile, away from sanctuary or temple. Now a "diet of tears" seems to be the daily menu (verse 4), his only portion as well as his libation. The prayer recalls the good days when he sought the living God, the face of God, as a lively participant in the cultic assembly at the house of God (verse 5). Now he is downcast; he gives himself a pep talk; the pray-er dialogues with himself and his God: there is hope and that hope is God. The refrain found in Psalm 42, verses 6 and 12, and Psalm 43, verse 5 gives a certain unity to these two psalms, which were originally one.

This psalm and verses 7-12 in particular ripple with references to water, often a symbol of disaster, foes, chaos. The river Jordan and its source, the melting snow from Mount Hermon, the roaring cataracts, the breakers and billows all pass over the psalmist, bringing him a steady "diet of tears." They generate a downcast and dismal state. And then comes the taunting question: "Where is your God?"

The "roar of the mighty waters" expresses the psalmist's state of near despair and disorientation. The tumult of the waves is comparable to a slap in the face by God, who seems to have abandoned his pray-er (verse 10). Sadness is not the answer. The psalmist continues to hope, to wait on God, for only God can bridge these troubled waters, these stormy seas that lash out against the life of this worshiper.

God is sanctuary. He is shelter, refuge, stronghold (Ps 43, 3f). All biblical prayer — particularly the psalms — follows a road and a path that eventually lead to the temple mount. All biblical prayer literally or in spirit winds up at the temple altar (verse 4), the holy mountain, God's dwelling place where the people seek the face of the Lord. Here the God of our life, the living God, resides.

ON THE NATURE OF PRAYER

God is sanctuary; God is shelter, refuge, and stronghold. There is a rich tradition of sanctuary in the Bible which is today becoming a relevant occupation as well as a dangerous one. Some churches in North America are taking great risks in offering asylum to their South and Central American brothers and sisters. Sanctuaries in the biblical tradition are life-giving and justice-seeking, and people who call themselves Christian must continue to foster them. Our homes and our churches must become shelters and asylums for the poor and dispossessed.

psalm 63

¹*A psalm of David, when he was in the wilderness of Judah.*

²O God, you are my God whom I seek;
    for you my flesh pines and my soul thirsts like the
    earth, parched, lifeless and without water.

3Thus have I gazed toward you in the sanctuary
      to see your power and your glory,
4For your kindness is a greater good than life;
      my lips shall glorify you.

5Thus will I bless you while I live;
      lifting up my hands, I will call upon your name.
6As with the riches of a banquet
      shall my soul be satisfied,
      and with exultant lips
      my mouth shall praise you.
7I will remember you upon my couch, and through the
      night-watches I will meditate on you:
8That you are my help,
      and in the shadow of your wings I shout for joy.
9My soul clings fast to you;
      your right hand upholds me.

10But they shall be destroyed who seek my life,
      they shall go into the depths of the earth;
11They shall be delivered over to the sword,
      and shall be the prey of jackals.
12The king, however, shall rejoice in God;
      everyone who swears by him shall glory,
      but the mouths of those who speak falsely
      shall be stopped.

The thirst for God (verse 2) and the longing for his sanctuary (verse 3) continue. The caption to this psalm speaks "of David, when he was in the wilderness of Judah."

The "wilderness" (desert) of Judah is in sharp contrast with the city Jerusalem, the oasis. City and desert — stark contrasts — stand adjacent to each other and offer space for meditation. It is often in the desert, seemingly devoid of life, that Israel learns about herself and about her God. The desert becomes Israel's classroom for an enrichment course on Yahweh. The desert suggests the edge of existence, the epicenter of angelic/demonic forces vying for our loyalty. The desert becomes the place of revelation and epiphanies as well as the locus of trials, temptations, and murmurings of the people. It is the place to frequent while at the same time the place to avoid. It is the residence of snakes and scorpions but also the seeding ground of miraculous births, blooming desert flowers, and glorious sunsets. Reminders of death as well as new ways of life surface in this arid spot that produces mirages, hallucinations, and miracles. Little things take on great importance in the desert. Drinking water, even if it's hot, becomes the "desert cocktail"; a tiny tamarisk bush has the appeal of a Lebanon cedar. Wild animals frolicking in the hot desert sand witness to the laws of evolution and survival of the fittest. Money, of value elsewhere, serves no purpose in the desert devoid of fast food chains and 7-Eleven counters. Desert hospitality is more important than "meet me at the Hilton." For safety's sake one learns to travel in groups in the desert, to trust, and to value tent fellowship. In essence one learns to depend on others and ultimately on God.

The nearness of the "city Jerusalem" to the "wilderness of Judah" is probably God's idea of geographical strategy as well as his idea of spiritual topography, intended to keep all of us honest in our search for him. We and Israel constantly live on the borders of the desert. Our God has a sense of humor.

From this circuitous and tortuous trek through the desert, we can arrive at the psalmist's appreciation for God's sanctuary (verse 3) and understand his opening words, "O God, you are my God, whom I seek; for you my flesh pines and my soul thirsts like the earth, parched, lifeless and without water" (verse 2). Scorched from the day's heat and life's battles, the psalmist seeks the shelter of "the shadow of your (God's) wings" (verse 8). There he will call upon the Lord's name (verse 5). One gets the impression that the pray-er will spend the night in the temple, an incubation rite that many practiced. Through the night watches one will meditate on the Lord as s/he remembers the Lord upon his couch (verse 7). In the closing verses 10-12, the pray-er hopes that all foes will be destroyed and become the prey of jackals.

On the Nature of Prayer
Desire and longing are prerequisites for anything important in life. A searching, zealous spirit, much like a thirsty person's desire for water, is a prayerful disposition and attitude. Prayer quenches your thirst for the Lord.

psalm 84

¹*For the leader; "upon the* gittith." *A psalm of the sons of Korah.*

²How lovely is your dwelling place, O Lord of hosts!
³My soul yearns and pines for the courts of the Lord.

My heart and my flesh cry out for the living God.
4Even the sparrow finds a home,
    and the swallow a nest
    in which she puts her young—
Your altars, O Lord of hosts,
    my king and my God!
5Happy they who dwell in your house!
    continually they praise you.
6Happy the men whose strength you are!
    their hearts are set upon the pilgrimage:
7When they pass through the valley of the mastic trees,
    they make a spring of it;
    the early rain clothes it with generous growth.
8They go from strength to strength;
    they shall see the God of gods in Zion.

9O LORD of hosts, hear my prayer;
    hearken, O God of Jacob!
10O God, behold our shield,
    and look upon the face of your anointed.
11I had rather one day in your courts
    than a thousand elsewhere;
I had rather lie at the threshold of the house of my God
    than dwell in the tents of the wicked.
12For a sun and a shield is the LORD God;
    grace and glory he bestows;
The Lord withholds no good thing
    from those who walk in sincerity.
13O LORD of hosts, happy the men who trust in you!

This psalm is somewhat similar to Psalms 42 and 43. Yet there are marked differences. The previous psalms suggest individual laments to express a longing for Jerusalem or some sanctuary. They give the impression that their hopes for an immediate visit to the shrine would not be forthcoming. Psalm 84 has a happier tone. A pilgrim song, it is sung enroute to Jerusalem, a song celebrating Zion which can be seen in the distance. As a canticle of Zion, it serves as an excellent transitional psalm to the grouping known as "pilgrim psalms" (120-134). It is a good "approach psalm" to Jerusalem and Zion. Proximity to Zion seems obvious.

The pilgrim anticipates above all else the loveliness of God's dwelling place (verse 2). For the pious Jew then and now, Zion is the emotional center of the universe, the navel of the world. Here God has pitched his tent and taken up residence. Happy are those who visit him, who call upon his name. The psalmist yearns for this as his soul, heart, and flesh cry out for the living God (verse

3). Such is the language of a poet, a mystic, or a lover who pines and waits for the arrival of the object of his or her affection. One's whole being is carried away. Just as the birds (sparrows and swallows) find a nest there, so does the pilgrim find shelter and refuge at the sanctuary. Bird talk becomes God talk. Just as the birds make joyful noises from their perches in the sanctuary, so will the temple singers chime forth from their choir lofts in praise of the living God, the God who is creator of all—birds and humans. Birds have their homing instincts (nests); so, too, do the pilgrims who come home to roost in the temple.

Happiness is the note and tenor of the pilgrim on the way (verses 5-8). Old Testament beatitudinal bliss marks the face of the weary and anxious traveler approaching Jerusalem and Zion, the holy hill.

Verses 7 and 8 create some difficulty as translators try to decide whether the Hebrew refers to the Baca Valley, the valley of tears and weeping, or to the Balsam Valley, a valley of aromatic delight where one gets a "whiff of salvation" emanating from the nearby city of salvation. Perhaps it is best to leave the meaning foggy since one's approach to Jerusalem, the hill of Zion and the hill of Calvary, will always be a mixed blessing, a bittersweet experience. Yet the city will offer comfort and consolation just as early gentle rains clothe the dry, parched earth (verse 7). Mere sight of this city, a source of joy and strength (verse 8), renews both body and spirit.

The lines in verses 9-13 resemble a prayer for the king sprinkled with expressions of trust in God, in life, for one day in God's presence—his court—is better than a thousand elsewhere. We are all familiar with ecstatic experiences, albeit few. One afternoon of October lovemaking makes us forget a thousand lonely hours. Being on the threshold of the house of someone we love is better than dwelling in the living room of one who is more foe than friend. We would all rather share a simple meal with a friend than engage in an orgy with a community of strangers. Such is our God, who withholds no good thing from those he loves (verse 12).

ON THE NATURE OF PRAYER

This "approach psalm" to Jerusalem, the city of salvation, reminds us to use all our senses while praying. The sight of the city on the horizon, the smell of the balsam trees in the Kidron Valley near the city where one gets a whiff of salvation, the sound of the arrival of chirping sparrow and swallow all remind us that our entire person, with all of our senses, is important in our quest for the living God. Author Edward Hays implores us to "pray through our noses," read Scripture "through our noses," especially the love poetry of the *Song of Songs*, for we are alive. The idols of the pagans are said to have mouths but speak not, eyes but see not, ears but hear not, noses but smell not (Ps 115: 5-6). Refrain from imitating these pagan idols, Hays reminds us. He urges us to fully employ all our senses, our voices especially, to give praise to the living God. The aromas, the fragrance, the olfactory delights of the Balsam Valley suggest that we are on the threshold of the Holy, in the vicinity of Jerusalem.

Creature as wayfarer:
pilgrim psalms
psalms 120-134

The happier tone of Psalm 84, a canticle of Zion, serves as an excellent transitional and introductory psalm to the grouping known as pilgrim, gradual, and ascents (Pss 120-134). The pilgrims sang these songs on annual visits for feasts in Jerusalem. They seem quite appropriate for a post-Vatican II Church of "pilgrim people" and "people of God." Just as those early pilgrims journeyed up to the earthly Jerusalem, so does the contemporary pilgrim set out toward the heavenly Jerusalem, always an uphill climb. At the same time, pilgrimages excite and exhilarate people.

psalm 122

¹*A song of ascents. Of David.*

I rejoiced because they said to me,
  "We will go up to the house of the Lord."
²And now we have set foot within your gates,
  O Jerusalem —
³Jerusalem, built as a city with compact unity.
⁴To it the tribes go up, the tribes of the Lord,
  according to the decree for Israel,
  to give thanks to the name of the Lord.
⁵In it are set up judgment seats,
  seats for the house of David.

⁶Pray for the peace of Jerusalem!
  May those who love you prosper!
⁷May peace be within your walls,
  prosperity in your buildings.
⁸Because of my relatives and friends
  I will say, "Peace be within you!"
⁹Because of the house of the Lord, our God,
  I will pray for your good.

This psalm is so akin in spirit to Psalm 84 that it merits mention here. The opening lines (verses 1-3) capture the emotional pitch of the group when they learn that pilgrimage time is near. In an age when there were no calendars, messengers or troubadours no doubt communicated good news of upcoming events. In a very short time, (verse 2) the pilgrims assembled at the gates of Jerusalem or even at the temple gates. Gatekeepers, questioning the pilgrims, tested their sincerity. The gates of the city and the temple are pivotal hinges for understanding several psalms. They serve as the entrance to the compact and unified city (verse 3) to keep the enemy out and make the inhabitants feel secure and safe. Gate liturgies are an important aspect of Jewish piety and spirituality. Gates are the visas and passports to shalom — well-being.

It is here that the tribes, the families, the sons of the covenant went up according to the decree prescribed for annual feasts (verses 4-6). It is here that priests and prophets did their teaching, where they gave their judgments on lawsuits and cases too difficult to handle elsewhere. Jerusalem at that time served as the Supreme Court and as Capitol Hill, since religious, national, and political concerns were of the same fabric. Sometimes abuses and corruption spoiled the pilgrimage attitude.

Peace, happiness, prosperity are manifestations of God's blessings; the very name Jerusalem suggests peace, shalom (verses 6-9). Even today in a war-torn Middle East, Jerusalem has a peaceful serenity unmatched by any other city in the world. Not even Arab and Israeli artillery can dispel the peace there.

psalm 127

¹*A song of ascents. Of Solomon.*

Unless the LORD build the house,
    they labor in vain who build it.
Unless the LORD guard the city,
    in vain does the guard keep vigil.
²It is vain for you to rise early, or put off your rest,
    you that eat hard-earned bread,
    for he gives to his beloved in sleep.

³Behold, sons are a gift from the LORD;
    the fruit of the womb is a reward.
⁴Like arrows in the hand of a warrior
    are the sons of one's youth.

⁵Happy the man whose quiver is filled with them;
they shall not be put to shame
when they contend with enemies at the gate.

This psalm stresses the blessings and value of family and community life, reflecting Israel's covenant relationship with her God. It does not deny human effort and cooperation, but it emphasizes the import of trust in God's help.

"Unless the Lord build the house, they labor in vain who build it" (verse 1). "House" suggests family, community, Israel, Church. The Lord is the builder and life-giver to these houses. Just as a sail cannot move a ship without the aid of a mysterious wind, so too no effective building can take place in the Scriptures without God as chief architect. Solomon, a great builder, is not remembered as a great king or person — his "edifice complex" caused him to build many projects via the forced labor of fellow Israelites. Lady Wisdom, however, is commended for building a house with strong pillars and foundation; she built with the Lord's blueprint in mind.

Verse 2 tells us it is vain to rise early or go to bed late if the Lord is not involved in the building plan. Both early birds and night owls are reprimanded if God is not included in the early day and night watches (vigils), designated times for Israelite prayer.

Israel should not worry or fret but should trust in God who gives his blessings while people sleep (verse 2b). He is the giver of the mysterious dew at night that is so crucial for plant and vegetative life, as well as the nightly dew which produces offspring. Conception was still considered a nighttime mystery.

Verses 3-5 prize the blessings of children, especially sons. The more sons in a family meant less worry about work in the fields or justice at the city gates. A father with many sons (arrows in his quiver) found strength in number. Many children also provided joy and support in old age and gave adult children the opportunity to live out the fourth commandment, "Honor your father and your mother" (Ex 20:12).

psalm 128

¹*A song of ascents.*

Happy are you who fear the Lᴏʀᴅ,
who walk in his ways!

²For you shall eat the fruit of your handiwork;
    happy shall you be, and favored.
³Your wife shall be like a fruitful vine
    in the recesses of your home;
 Your children like olive plants
    around your table.
⁴Behold, thus is the man blessed
    who fears the LORD.

⁵The LORD bless you from Zion:
    may you see the prosperity of Jerusalem
    all the days of your life;
⁶May you see your children's children.
    Peace be upon Israel!

Yet another pilgrim psalm describes the joys of domestic life, almost consciously continuing the thought of the previous song about children as "a gift from the Lord" and "fruit of the womb."

Happiness is linked with "fear of the Lord" (verse 1). This typical advice from the sage guarantees results if it is obeyed.

We read in verses 2 and 3 that "fear of the Lord" shall bear fruit, food for the table, and children, the fruit of the womb. The wife — the fruitful vine — will see her children gathered like olive plants around the table. Table talk, family talk, and God talk dovetail. Covenant and table fellowship join hands in prayer. This positive, idealistic psalm dwells upon the rewards of "fear of the Lord": a loving wife and children. Love and fertility is contagious, passed on from generation to generation, to one's children's children (verse 6) and beyond. Progeny is a sign of primordial blessing in Scripture (Gn 1: 28), and progeny along with land continue to be the main story line of the promises to Abraham and the patriarchal narratives. Nearly every page of Scripture narrates a birth or two.

Children spell divine gift and blessing. Children inkle immortality in Old Testament times, for their elders live on in them. The opposite of this blessing is a curse, barrenness. What then of the barren woman, the sterile husband, and obstacles to fertility? Some of the most famous women in Scripture (Sarah, Rebekah, Rachel, Hannah, to name a few) were barren. Are we to consider them accursed and punished by God? By no means. Rather, they symbolize potent receptacles who witness to an active passivity, a waiting upon the Lord for his word and for his seed to become manifest, fertile, and fruitful in their lives. All of these women eventually give birth to an important person in the salvific process with God as chief architect and midwife. Our God has a strange sense of humor and of "planned parenthood."

psalm 133

¹*A song of ascents. Of David.*

> Behold, how good it is, and how pleasant,
>   where brethren dwell at one!
> ²It is as when the precious ointment upon the head
>   runs down over the beard, the beard of Aaron,
>   till it runs down upon the collar of his robe.
> ³It is a dew like that of Hermon,
>   which comes down upon the mountains of Zion;
> For there the LORD has pronounced his blessing,
>   life forever.

This "pilgrim psalm" extols family life and community. Its brevity should not deceive us. Those of us who live in community know that this mystery cannot be dismissed in three short verses. Today's trend toward a breakdown in family order and structure and more and more suspicion about community living causes us to pause and give this short psalm our attention.

It is good and pleasant when people can dwell at one, in unity. The attitude with which a community or family member prays verse 1 tells us much about that person. Is such a lofty ideal cynical or is it a realizable goal? In reality, when and where family and community exist, it is a blessing.

Verse 2 tells us that unity is like precious ointment upon the head that runs down over Aaron's beard and onto the collar of his robe. Oil (precious ointment) signifies divine blessing. Anyone who has lived in the Middle East appreciates and knows the value of oil. Oil is used as a condiment and for cosmetic purposes. It has medicinal qualities that heal wounds; it is an ingredient in perfumes; it is also used as a fragrant oil for anointing cultic personnel, particularly the high priest, hence the reason for the name Aaron. This ceremonial ointment was generously poured over the head of the anointed (which "messiah" means). The rule of thumb negated a "little dab will do" mentality. On the contrary, lavish and generous outpourings of oil would inundate the anointed one from the top of the head, down his neck, onto the

beard and then onto the collar of his robes. This scene is comparable to our modern custom of pouring champagne over the win-
ners in sporting events such as the World Series or the Super
Bowl. The anointed one is literally the smeared one who is lavish-
ly blessed.

The rich heavenly dew (verse 3) expresses the blessing of family unity. This mysterious morning dew from heaven is refresh-
ing, invigorating. It is a God-sent blessing so desperately needed
in a dry, parched land with little water. Mount Hermon in the
north is a snow-capped peak, a region noted for its heavy dew,
and the source of the River Jordan. As the oil descended onto
Aaron's beard, so does the dew descend upon the hill of Zion, object of the Lord's blessing.

Three times in this psalm blessings descend upon family life,
and the result of these blessings is life forever. The fostering,
preservation, and prolongation of earthly life were the functions
of the family; there was no firm belief in a life hereafter at that
time. Living on through one's children often depicted immortality. Life forever was a way of saying that good things like family
and community life should never end. No one likes to see good
things come to an end.

In summary, dew, the mysterious mist in early morning, is
necessary for oil-producing plants. Without it, both land and
people wither. In using these images of oil and dew, the psalmist
suggests that happy family life is a blend of elements planned (human effort) and mysterious, elements unplanned (divine blessings). Familial happiness and unity depend upon people and
upon God, upon heaven and earth, upon the human and the divine. One has to work at it and pray for it, but it is also a gift
from above.

ON THE NATURE OF PRAYER
On this earthly pilgrimage of ours, life and prayer will always go
together. Family life will demand family prayer since we pray our
experiences and experience our prayers. Prayer will always be familial, communal, a social and public act and witness. This psalm
may idealize the family situation but prayer will always tease us
into a possible and realizable future.

This psalm invites us to taste the blessings of harmony among
members of our own family, our community, and the families of
others. We need to savor the unity among diverse peoples: be-

tween Israel and the Church, between the churched and the unchurched, and among all peoples in the global village. Oil is needed but so also is the dew.

In addition to the pilgrim psalms (120-134), the Canticles of Zion such as 46, 48, 76, 84, and 87 have a journey motif.

Liturgical creatures
psalms 15 and 24

psalm 15

¹*A psalm of David.*

O Lord, who shall sojourn in your tent?
    Who shall dwell on your holy mountain?

²He who walks blamelessly and does justice;
    who thinks the truth in his heart
³   and slanders not with his tongue;
    Who harms not his fellow man,
        nor takes up a reproach against his neighbor;
⁴By whom the reprobate is despised,
    while he honors those who fear the LORD;
Who, though it be to his loss,
    changes not his pledged word;
⁵   who lends not his money at usury
    and accepts no bribe against the innocent.

He who does these things shall never be disturbed.

psalm 24

¹*A psalm of David.*

The LORD's are the earth and its fullness;
    the world and those who dwell in it.
²For he founded it upon the seas
    and established it upon the rivers.

³Who can ascend the mountain of the LORD?
    or who may stand in his holy place?
⁴He whose hands are sinless, whose heart is clean,
    who desires not what is vain,
        nor swears deceitfully to his neighbor.
⁵He shall receive a blessing from the LORD,
    a reward from God his savior.

⁶Such is the race that seeks for him,
    that seeks the face of the God of Jacob.

⁷Lift up, O gates, your lintels;
    reach up, you ancient portals,
    that the king of glory may come in!
⁸Who is this king of glory?
    The LORD, strong and mighty,
    the LORD, mighty in battle.
⁹Lift up, O gates, your lintels;
    reach up, you ancient portals,
    that the king of glory may come in!
¹⁰Who is this king of glory?
    The LORD of hosts; he is the king of glory.

These two psalms or entrance hymns are similar. They describe the questioning that the pilgrims experienced when they arrived at the city or temple gates. Elsewhere (Ps 122: 2) we mentioned the import of gate liturgies among the Hebrews. To them comings and goings were crucial and often a sign of life or death. Today we still speak of entrance into the gates of heaven or the gates of hell. Salvation continues to hinge on access to some gates and closure to others.

"Who shall dwell on your holy mountain?" (Ps 15: 1) and "Who can ascend the mountain of the Lord or who may stand in his holy place?" (Ps 24: 3). Upon their arrival at the door of the temple, some cultic official, it seems, questioned the pilgrims. The official, a gatekeeper or Levite, tested the motivation and sincerity of those seeking entry. These prerequisites to enter for worship (Ps 15: 2-5 and Ps 24: 4) centered around moral qualities that emphasized social, communal, corporate concerns more than individual piety or private concerns. Questions of justice, truth, and charity were important. The process anticipates the New Testament exhortation to "make peace with one's neighbor before approaching the altar," for all sacrifice is odoriferous unless it is accompanied by the proper dispositions of justice and charity. All liturgy and sacrifice is related to treatment of our neighbor (Ps 15: 3) and symbolizes at-one-ment with God and with the worshiping community. These entrance requirements stem from the Torah, the heart of the Jewish Scriptures. They are appropriate as an examination of conscience at the gate or door (Tor in German) of the temple. Torah testing at the Tor is the price of admission and one's passport to the inner sanctuary and inner life with God.

Psalm 24: 7-10 makes reference to the ark carried in procession to the gates of the temple. Just as the pilgrim approaching the gates asks for admission, so do the cultic personnel carrying the ark (God's presence) dialogue with the gatekeepers to seek the ark's entrance. The pilgrim may have been unworthy and fallen short of the entrance requirements; the ark (presence of God) by contrast is so great and so tall that the lintels and portals of the holy temple itself may not be able to contain its majestic presence. The dialogic nature of these verses hold clues to the psalm's liturgical use. Alternating groups of the worshiping community provide the text or lyrics that accompany this ritual procession with the ark.

ON THE NATURE OF PRAYER:
Prayer and sacrifice always make moral demands. Life with God and life with neighbor are interlocked. A generous and gracious spirit opens doors while a selfish nature closes doors in our life with God and with one another. In prayer we open the doors of our hearts to let the ark (God's presence) enter and take up residence.

Psalms 132 and 134 also include some liturgical aspects.

Worshiping creatures: enthronement psalms 93, 96, 97, 99

The four concluding verses of the previous processional Psalm 24 lead very well into the category of psalms known as enthronement psalms. We treat this cluster of psalms in a general way while noting their common salient features.

The setting of these psalms is the cult, perhaps an enthronement festival. The central figure is Yahweh as king; the chief concern is his kingship. It is important to emphasize that this class of psalms deals with royalty (God's). They differ from the royal psalms which are deeply rooted in court life and deal with events and experiences of the earthly king of Israel or Judah (see royal psalms).

"The LORD is King": This familiar shout normally used to acknowledge a new king appears in Psalms 93, 97, 99. It demonstrates that the king and kingship were truly treasured in the ancient Near East. Early in its history, Israel sought to initiate kingship. As is true with many new proposals, the people had many misgivings since up to now they considered Yahweh alone as Israel's king. Israel should not stoop to become like other nations who embodied their gods in earthly rulers. Israel was different; it was to remain different. But the political pressures overwhelmed her and her constituents, and eventually Israel opted for a king like other nations. Safety and security lay in kingship.

In the cult, however, Yahweh alone is king. His rule of universal scope was something Israel's earthly rulers did not achieve. His kingship includes the present but also extends into the future. This is acted out in the cult.

After the pilgrims' arrival at the gate of the temple and the questioning process that took place (Pss 15 and 24), they witnessed the advent, the coming of God in the presence of the ark; now they were ready to enthrone him and proclaim his sovereignty over them. They were about to begin the installation of God.

psalm 93

¹The Lord is king, in splendor robed;
　　robed is the Lord and girt about with strength;
And he has made the world firm, not to be moved.
²Your throne stands firm from of old;
　　from everlasting you are, O Lord.

³The floods lift up, O Lord, the floods lift up their voice;
　　the floods lift up their tumult.
⁴More powerful than the roar of many waters,
　　more powerful than the breakers of the sea —
　　powerful on high is the Lord.
⁵Your decrees are worthy of trust indeed:
　　holiness befits your house, O Lord,
　　for length of days.

The king acclaimed in these enthronement psalms is to have power over the waters, floods, and chaos in general (verses 3 and 4). The curbing and calming of waters and the ordering of primeval waters were traits attributed to ancient Near Eastern kings. The taming of waters often figures into the creation stories told during these times. This demonstrates that God, the King, is in control. This control over waters also suggests the saving act of God at the sea during the Exodus. Many of the psalms praising the king have nature and creation, history and redemption, liturgy and cult joining together to give praise to the Lord enthroned on high.

psalm 96

¹Sing to the Lord a new song;
　　sing to the Lord, all you lands.
²Sing to the Lord, bless his name;
　　announce his salvation, day after day.
³Tell his glory among the nations;
　　among all peoples, his wondrous deeds.

⁴For great is the Lord and highly to be praised;
　　awesome is he, beyond all gods.
⁵For all the gods of the nations are things of nought,
　　but the Lord made the heavens.
⁶Splendor and majesty go before him;
　　praise and grandeur are in his sanctuary.

⁷Give to the Lord, you families of nations,
　　give to the Lord glory and praise;

8   give to the Lᴏʀᴅ the glory due his name!
Bring gifts, and enter his courts;
9   worship the Lᴏʀᴅ in holy attire.
Tremble before him, all the earth;
10   say among the nations: The Lᴏʀᴅ is king.
He has made the world firm, not to be moved;
        he governs the peoples with equity.

11Let the heavens be glad and the earth rejoice;
        let the sea and what fills it resound;
12   let the plains be joyful and all that is in them!
Then shall all the trees of the forest exult
13   before the Lᴏʀᴅ, for he comes;
        for he comes to rule the earth.
He shall rule the world with justice
        and the peoples with his constancy.

The opening verses (1-3) capture another feature of the enthronement psalms celebrating Yahweh as King. They have a
universal ring that invites all lands, all nations, and all peoples to
sing a new song; that is, yet another song, since our God is so
great and awesome (verses 4-6) that no one song can contain his
greatness. This universal thrust continues in verses 7-10; let all
peoples proclaim "The LORD is king." In verses 11-13 all nature
and creation — earth, sea, plains, trees of the forest — join together
their joyful sounds at the sight of the Lord's coming. All creation
rejoices in God as King.

psalm 97

1The Lᴏʀᴅ is king; let the earth rejoice;
        let the many isles be glad.
2Clouds and darkness are round about him, justice and
        judgment are the foundation of his throne.
3Fire goes before him
        and consumes his foes round about.
4His lightnings illumine the world;
        the earth sees and trembles.
5The mountains melt like wax before the Lᴏʀᴅ,
        before the Lᴏʀᴅ of all the earth.
6The heavens proclaim his justice,
        and all peoples see his glory.

7All who worship graven things are put to shame,
        who glory in the things of nought;
        all gods are prostrate before him.

8Zion hears and is glad, and the cities of Judah rejoice
    because of your judgments, O Lord.
9Because you, O Lord, are the Most High over all the
    earth, exalted far above all gods.
10The Lord loves those that hate evil;
    he guards the lives of his faithful ones;
    from the hand of the wicked he delivers them.
11Light dawns for the just;
    and gladness, for the upright of heart.
12Be glad in the Lord, you just,
    and give thanks to his holy name.

This psalm opens with a theophany or appearance of the Lord
within the cult (verses 1-6). God manifests himself amid clouds,
darkness, fire, lightning; the earth trembles and the mountains
melt like wax at the awesome sight of the Lord. Cosmic upheavals
often accompany God's coming, inducing both fright and awe.
Nature responds with claps of joy or shrieks of fright to the mystery of God's presence. This scene is reminiscent of Sinai, the
mountain where Moses encountered God's presence in the burn-
ing bush. Here in the cult, both nature and history, important in
God's salvific plan, lend praise to the Lord. Creation theology
comes together with salvation history.

When the Lord comes, the just judge will parcel out justice to
all. Those who worship graven things or idols will be brought to
shame, while everything and everyone will bow down to praise
the Lord, customary in the cult.

psalm 99

1The Lord is king; the peoples tremble;
    he is throned upon the cherubim;
    the earth quakes.
2The Lord in Zion is great,
    he is high above all the peoples.
3Let them praise your great and awesome name;
    holy is he!

4The King in his might loves justice;
    you have established equity;
    justice and judgment in Jacob you have wrought.
5   Extol the Lord, our God,
    and worship at his footstool;
    holy is he!

> 6Moses and Aaron were among his priests,
>   and Samuel, among those
>   who called upon his name;
>   they called upon the LORD, and he answered them.
> 7From the pillar of cloud he spoke to them;
>   they heard his decrees and the law he gave them.
> 8O LORD, our God, you answered them;
>   a forgiving God you were to them,
>   though requiting their misdeeds.
> 9   Extol the LORD, our God,
>   and worship at his holy mountain;
>   for holy is the LORD, our God.

This last enthronement psalm begins with the familiar shout "The LORD is king!" This psalm accentuates the holiness of this God King, and the community response is awe. The peoples tremble, the earth quakes, a response common in other biblical theophanies (verses 1-3). This appearance of the Lord is in the cult. The King God is praised as a lover of justice and equity (verses 4-5). The tradition and spirit of Moses, Aaron, and Samuel still live on in the worshiping community. Just as the Lord spoke to these heroes in the faith long ago, so does he now speak in and to the worshiping community—a community of priests. The language of these verses (6-9) is again theophanic so it becomes difficult to distinguish the great appearances of the Lord in history from those now occurring in the cult. Past and present fuse in cult and liturgy. The overarching unity is the presence of the Eternal One, King, and God. Let us worship at his holy mountain.

ON THE NATURE OF PRAYER

These enthronement psalms witness to God's coming presence and installation as king among his people. They capture the spirit of Advent in ancient Israel. God is still coming, still appearing in our midst, and in our assemblies when we gather for worship and prayer. We too enthrone the King of kings when we gather for praise. This God makes his home, his abode, his palace among the praises of Israel and of the Church.

Psalm 47 is often included with the above cluster of enthronement psalms in honor of Yahweh's kingship.

Royal psalms:
theology fit for a king
psalm 2

¹Why do the nations rage
  and the peoples utter folly?
²The kings of the earth rise up,
  and the princes conspire together
  against the LORD and against his anointed:
³"Let us break their fetters
  and cast their bonds from us!"

⁴He who is throned in heaven laughs;
  the LORD derides them.
⁵Then in anger he speaks to them;
  he terrifies them in his wrath:
⁶"I myself have set up my king on Zion,
  my holy mountain."

⁷I will proclaim the decree of the LORD:
  The Lord said to me, "You are my son;
  this day I have begotten you.
⁸Ask of me and I will give you
  the nations for an inheritance
  and the ends of the earth for your possession.
⁹You shall rule them with an iron rod;
  you shall shatter them like an earthen dish."

¹⁰And now, O kings, give heed;
  take warning, you rulers of the earth.
¹¹Serve the LORD with fear, and rejoice before him;
¹²   with trembling pay homage to him,
  lest he be angry and you perish from the way,
  when his anger blazes suddenly.
  Happy are all who take refuge in him!

The enthronement psalms extol Yahweh as king and their setting is in the cult, while the royal psalms extol the earthly kings of
Israel or Judah and their setting is in courtly life.

Since both groups of psalms focus on images of kingship, there
was often confusion. The earthly king was alleged to be tall, hand-

some, and potent; this led the people to sometimes confuse Yahweh with a fertility deity. Likewise, the avowed earthly king was a
brave warrior, a defender of justice and rights, and the people mis-
takenly made Yahweh a god of war and developed a "holy war"
mentality. Since the earthly king's domain was law and cult in addition to war, his leadership strayed to temple abuses, tyrannical
abuses, and corruption.

It was easy to confuse the house of God—the temple—with the
adjacent palace of the king. It was easy to let the incense offered
to God in the cult become blurred with the affection and the ad-
miration the people displayed for the reigning monarch. It was
easy, too, to equate God's will with the direction, advice, and
counsel of the king. In short, it was often easy to confuse the
ways of God and the ways of man. Kingship in Israel could be a
drawback as well as an asset. The reign of both Yahweh and the
earthly king was supposedly of universal scope and when things
went right, all rejoiced. But when they went sour, the people experienced much misery in the kingdom of God and in the king-
doms of Israel and Judah.

Royal psalms—Pss 2, 20, 21, 45, 72, 101 and 110—commemo-
rate various events in a king's life: his coronation, his going into
battle, his wedding, his oath of office, his anniversary of coronation. The king, the recipient of God's gifts and blessings, chan-
neled these same blessings to the people. God blessed and gifted
David more than any other person or king. He made covenant
with David's house and dynasty, a kingdom that was to last forever. In some way the king embodied the entire people; a corporate personality was on display and the people acclaimed the king
as God's anointed or Messiah. The hopes of Israel resided in the
king. A king in Israel or Judah meant there was hope for the nation and the people, as well as the hope for a messianic era. But at
the time of the Babylonian exile when kingship vanished, many
of these hopes were shattered. Yet the people in the postexilic era
continued to sing, pray, and hope in these royal psalms even
when kingship had succumbed to new pressures and new demands. Thus these psalms commemorating historical regal events
took on a futuristic character, looking toward a more distant
time. Singing and praying royal psalms after the exile was Israel's
way of staying alive spiritually—her way of hoping. Hope was
always a code word for God who was future as well as present to
Israel.

While the enthronement psalms spoke of God's installation as king, this royal psalm speaks of the installation or coronation of an earthly king. On this day God's elect and chosen one, the king, becomes God's son, his adopted son (verse 7).

The opening verses (1-3) give the impression that there was much unrest and even revolt when the throne was vacant. These interregnum periods could be times of turmoil and much jockeying for position. But the Lord would do it his way (verses 4-6). He laughs at the scuffling and makes it known who is really king of Zion. Why all the confusion over who is really king?

Then some cultic official representing God declares in oracular form that this king — this man — is God's son, his adopted son, his chosen one (verse 7). The king's birthday as son of God is the king's coronation day. That day a son is born *of* God, a son is born *to* God. It is understandable that these so-called royal psalms took on messianic overtones in the course of time. By hindsight, they were especially applicable to Christ, the Messiah, the Anointed One. Transmitting power to the new king came through his anointing, through the action of smearing him with oil.

The newly designated king gets the promise of blessings and success; his rule will extend over all the earth (verse 8). This sounds like Semite hyperbole since Israel's or Judah's kings didn't ever enjoy such extensive sovereignty. A "kinglet" was a more appropriate title in most cases. Nevertheless, the royal ideology is important here in a theology fit for a king.

Thus other kings and vassals should take heed (verse 10) and acknowledge the true king (verse 12) chosen by God himself and announced via messianic decree by a designated cultic official. The psalm ends on a happy note — a beatitudinal note — for as the king goes, so goes Israel or Judah. If a king is enthroned, then there is hope for all of Israel. The king represents all the people; he is their mediator between heaven and earth, their bridgebuilder between God's house in the heavens and God's house on earth in the temple. The more the earthly king mirrors and images Yahweh, the heavenly king, the more Israel is like God. The more they live out the covenant they made with David, the more blessed Israel will be.

ON THE NATURE OF PRAYER:
What can royal psalms teach us about prayer since we have little or no contact with kings and royalty? Prayer can help us sort out

the chaff from our lives, sift out the genuine from the phony, the real from the pseudo. Israel had to sort, sift out, and discern God's will from the will of crafty, cunning, manipulative persons in power. So, too, does the contemporary believer have to make decisions, often independently from advice of seniors, counselors, people in power and authority who may not have God's will as their foremost priority. Often the pray-ers must combat contemporary pharaohs who would lord it over them. Prayer is a protest against unjust rule and rulers. It can no longer be an excuse to avoid working for justice. The real enemies are still the powers and principalities, the dark forces at work in and among us. Allegiance to the true King of kings is still a discerning task.

On the positive side, God mediates himself through the human, through the person of a king or another human being who has the immense responsibility to bridge heaven and earth and make us all royal persons, God's intention at creation. The evangelists put this psalm to use at Jesus' baptism or installation into his ministry when he was initiated into the mysterious divine life with his Father.

Many other royal psalms exist, namely: 18, 20, 21, 45, 72, 89, 101, 110, 132, 144.

Creatures of praise
psalm 104

¹Bless the LORD, O my soul!
 O LORD, my God, you are great indeed!
You are clothed with majesty and glory,
² robed in light as with a cloak.
You have spread out the heavens like a tent-cloth;
³ you have constructed your palace
 upon the waters.
You make the clouds your chariot;
 you travel on the wings of the wind.
⁴You make the winds your messengers,
 and flaming fire your ministers.

⁵You fixed the earth upon its foundation,
 not to be moved forever;
⁶With the ocean, as with a garment, you covered it;
 above the mountains the waters stood.
⁷At your rebuke they fled,
 at the sound of your thunder they took to flight;
⁸As the mountains rose, they went down the valleys
 to the place you had fixed for them.
⁹You set a limit they may not pass,
 nor shall they cover the earth again.

¹⁰You send forth springs into the watercourses
 that wind among the mountains,
¹¹And give drink to every beast of the field,
 till the wild asses quench their thirst.
¹²Beside them the birds of heaven dwell;
 from among the branches
 they send forth their song.
¹³You water the mountains from your palace;
 the earth is replete with the fruit of your works.
¹⁴You raise grass for the cattle,
 and vegetation for men's use,
 producing bread from the earth,
¹⁵ and wine to gladden men's hearts,
 so that their faces gleam with oil,
 and bread fortifies the hearts of men.

¹⁶Well watered are the trees of the LORD,
    the cedars of Lebanon, which he planted;
¹⁷In them the birds build their nests;
    fir trees are the home of the stork.
¹⁸The high mountains are for wild goats;
    the cliffs are a refuge for rock-badgers.

¹⁹You made the moon to mark the seasons;
    the sun knows the hour of its setting.
²⁰You bring darkness, and it is night;
    then all the beasts of the forest roam about;
²¹Young lions roar for the prey
    and seek their food from God.
²²When the sun rises, they withdraw
    and couch in their dens.
²³Man goes forth to his work
    and to his tillage till the evening.

²⁴How manifold are your works, O LORD!
    In wisdom you have wrought them all—
    the earth is full of your creatures;
²⁵The sea also, great and wide,
    in which are schools without number
    of living things both small and great,
²⁶And where ships move about with Leviathan,
    which you formed to make sport of it.

²⁷They all look to you
    to give them food in due time.
²⁸When you give it to them, they gather it;
    when you open your hand,
²⁹If you hide your face, they are dismayed;
    if you take away their breath,
    they perish and return to their dust.
³⁰When you send forth your spirit, they are created,
    and you renew the face of the earth.

³¹May the glory of the LORD endure forever;
    may the LORD be glad in his works!
³²He who looks upon the earth, and it trembles;
    who touches the mountains, and they smoke!
³³I will sing to the LORD all my life;
    I will sing praise to my God while I live.
³⁴Pleasing to him be my theme;
    I will be glad in the LORD.
³⁵May sinners cease from the earth,
    and may the wicked be no more.
    Bless the LORD, O my soul!
    Alleluia.

Someone once said that all religions begin with wonder and awe and are linked to nature and creation (see Ps 29). Religion instructors have the obligation to inculcate a sense of wonder in their students. The order, variety, and beauty of all creation becomes a credo for belief and witness. Not to believe in wonders or ceasing to believe in wonders borders on sin, according to the biblical view.

This psalm praises God our creator. All creation, all life, is attributed to Yahweh, the Eternal Architect, the Ground of our Being, himself grounded in creation theology. This most magnificent hymn is steeped in wonder. S. Terrien has referred to the "Lord of seven wonders" when commenting on this psalm. These seven wonders run closely parallel to the first account of creation (Gn 1). The wonders of the heavens (sky), earth, waters, vegetation, sun, moon, sea, and all life (all creatures) join in orchestrated praise to delight in creation. Heaven and earth—from top to bottom, head to toe, God's body—praise creation.

If creation is God's body, then that body is clothed with majesty and glory (verse 1) and robed in light as with a cloak. Like a desert nomad he spreads out the heavens like a tent-cloth (verse 2). This is amazing since it always takes more than one person to pitch a tent. This God of ours is awesome and truly wonder-full. This wonderful God makes his presence felt in wind and fire (verses 3-4), mysterious primal elements. One hears the whistling of the wind but can't see it; one hears the crackling of the fire but can't understand it. Wind and fire capture the spirit and ardor of God's mysterious presence in our lives, in all of creation. He is all around us but we fail to perceive his presence. The clothing, robes, and garb of God tend to conceal him as well as reveal him. He teases us with the gradual unveiling of his voluptuous nature. His flaming fire (lightning) blinds some, illuminates others. Our attitude and disposition toward creation is so important. Will we continue to rule over it or will we cooperate with nature and creation, since we are dealing with God's body?

In verses 5-9 God fixes limits to the earth and the waters when he separates the dry land from the waters, similar to the creation story (Gn 1). Creation witnesses to God's orders. According to the Bible, creation means putting order into chaos; the taming of ocean waters is a sign of God's victory over the waters (chaos). Waters know their place since he fixes their limits with his word (verse 7). God is in control.

These once fierce waters, now tamed, serve a good purpose as springs that give drink to all living creatures (verses 10-13). Water helps to produce grass for the cattle and vegetation for human use (verse 14); it also produces grain (bread), wine, and oil — three basics of life. The rivers and streams feed the fields and trees. They, in turn, feed other living creatures. In verses 10-18 we witness the biblical version of an intricate eco-system, an ecological balance, where nature, animals, and creatures live in peaceful coexistence and harmony, echoing the spirit of Isaiah 11: 6-9 when wolf and lamb lie down together. Awareness of the interconnectedness of all life on earth is manifest. This near idyllic harmony, hinting of a return to Eden, holds an interesting challenge for all of us in this late twentieth century as we try desperately to get in touch with nature and Mother Earth to pay her due homage.

God's ongoing providential care is for all of life, be it large life or small, prized life or puzzling life such as stork, wild goat, and rock badger. What purpose do they serve? This God teaches us to celebrate the useless (verses 17-18). What beauty, what variety, what order!

This wonderful God is not limited to earth. He also controls the sun and moon, the night and the day (verses 19-23). He is mightier than the Egyptian sun god, Ra, who must retire at night; our God does not die at night. Night is a time for wild beasts and for God.

Our wonderful God governs the seas and even its monsters (verses 24-26). God tames this chaos, sports with it, plays with it, makes it his pet.

But the real gem from the ocean of God's creation is the human creature (verses 27-30) who navigates through life as God's image, a combination of dust and divine breath. This human creature owes its entire dependence upon God, creator of all life and Ground of All Being. God's creation, not a one-time affair from the long-distant past, is an ongoing phenomenon. God's spirit still permeates the face of the earth.

Because of all this, we praise this God of ours (verses 31-35) who never ceases to amaze us, who never ceases to cause us to wonder. He is the reason for song, praise, and joy. He is the source of original blessing. Gladness radiates.

The last verse calls for eliminating sinners and the wicked. This may come as a surprise and a misfit in this beautiful and positive hymn about creation. But since sin is often viewed as an undoing of creation in the Scriptures, it fits well here. It may serve a significant purpose calling attention to the real presence of sin and evil in a basically good and friendly world. Likewise, it is an effective reminder that most of the time life and creation beckon to us with goodness, blessing, and gladness. From the very beginning, God saw that creation was very good. Let us delight in it and in him.

On the Nature of Prayer

Prayer and a sense of wonder go hand in hand. Prayer and religion develop a capacity for wonder, for rebirths, new creations. Nature helps us pray. Its wonders of the earth, skies, and seas are incentives to poets, lovers, contemplatives, and pilgrims. The Ground of All Being has his roots in creation which reminds us to praise him.

Psalm 104 is just one of many psalms of praise, in fact the entire psalter is a "Book of Praises." Psalms imbued with praise are: 8, 19, 29, 33, 100, 103, 111, 113, 114, 117, 135, 136, 145, 146, 147, 148, 149, 150.

Doxology
psalm 150

¹*Alleluia.*

Praise the LORD in his sanctuary,
 praise him in the firmament of his strength.
²Praise him for his mighty deeds,
 praise him for his sovereign majesty.
³Praise him with the blast of the trumpet,
 praise him with lyre and harp,
⁴Praise him with timbrel and harp,
 praise him with strings and pipe.
⁵Praise him with sounding cymbals,
 praise him with clanging cymbals.
⁶Let everything that has breath praise the LORD! Alleluia.

Psalm 150 with its emphasis on praise serves as an appropriate accompanying bookend with Psalm 1, an invitation to become the most happy creature. "Happy" and "Alleluia" (praise the Lord) mark the beginning and the end of the psalms, while those making up the middle part of the psalter are given to limits, to suffering, to laments — truly a parallel with life itself. It is in prayer that we do indeed pray our experiences, and in life we experience our prayers.

This final psalm is a fitting conclusion to the entire psalter, a book of hymns of praise. This doxology along with other mini-doxologies scattered throughout the psalter (see conclusions of Pss 41, 72, 89, 106) conclude the various books of the Psalms. The division of the psalter into five books seems to be analagous with the five books of Moses and was probably used in conjunction with them at temple and synagogal services.

This doxology is the last movement in the psalter's symphony of praise. A full orchestra — trumpet, lyre, harp, timbrel, strings, pipes, cymbals, and dance — is instrumental in praising the Lord of the performing arts. Good liturgy always demands good music, artistry, dance, and joyful sounds. Just as there is a variety of instruments, so also variety and diversity abound among worshipers, indicating that there can be unity amid diversity and that even cacophony can be recycled into polyphonic music pleasing to the ear. Liturgy, like God, tames the chaos of our lives. A new chemistry and a new web of relationships evolve when we bring words, sounds, music, movement, and ritual together. Our God can be a boisterous God who delights in joyful noises.

Good liturgy also reminds us that we don't leave our bodies at the door when we enter a temple or church to worship (the Hebrews learned this from their pagan neighbors). Our bodies participate in praising God, for good liturgy allows for bodily expression of soul. The entire person is invited to praise the Lord. Everything that has breath (verse 6) or wind, — reeds, pipes, humans — is instrumental in praising God. The liturgy should encourage a playful, spontaneous atmosphere.

Good liturgy needs constant updating; these ancient prayers should take on the spirit of age. The Psalms will always serve as a means to trigger new euphonic sonic booms, raw material even for the space age. Anthony St. Pierre, O.S.B., a physicist confrere, has made an adaptation of Psalm 150. He calls it "A Modern Canticle of Praise." It illustrates how the Psalms of old can inspire the prayer of an artist and scientist.

A Modern Canticle of Praise

> Praise him with laser and holograph,
> Praise him with color and charm,
> Praise him with blasts from the sonic boom,
> Praise him with drugs and dynamos,
> Praise him with storage rings and carbon rods,
> Praise him with betatrons and synchrotrons,
> Praise him with colliding beams.
> All you fundamental particles,
> sing and dance in your chambers.
> All you spins and dipoles,
> line up before the Lord.
> Let everything that is, praise Yahweh.
> Alleluia.

ON THE NATURE OF PRAYER

Once again temple sanctuary (cult), nature, and history (verses 1-2) join as one in contributing to prayer. All of Psalm 150 is an invitation to praise, yet the psalmist enumerates no motivations for praise. He seems to say that, having enrolled in the school of prayer, you learned to pray the first 149 psalms well. There is no further need, then, for explanation or motivation. You now know why we praise the Lord.

Alleluia!

Minidoxologies dot the psalter at the conclusion of Psalms 41, 72, 89, and 106, which along with Psalm 150 constitute "Five books of psalms" to match the "Five books of Moses" read in the temple and synagogues throughout the ages.

Suggested Reading

Anderson, Bernhard W., *Out of the Depths: The Psalms Speak for Us Today*. Philadelphia: Westminster Press, 1974.

Brueggemann, Walter, *In Man We Trust: The Neglected Side of Biblical Faith*. Atlanta: John Knox Press, 1972.

——————, *Praying the Psalms*. Winona, Minn.: St. Mary's Press, 1982.

Drijvers, Pius, *The Psalms: Their Structure and Meaning*. New York: Herder and Herder, 1965.

Fox, Matthew, *Original Blessing*. Santa Fe, N.Mex.: Bear & Co., Inc., 1983.

Gélin, Albert, *The Psalms Are Our Prayers*. Collegeville, Minn.: The Liturgical Press, 1964.

Guthrie, Harvey H., *Israel's Sacred Songs*. New York: Seabury Press, 1966.

Keel, Othmar, *The Symbolism of the Biblical World: Ancient Near Eastern Iconography and the Book of Psalms*. New York: Crossroads, 1978.

Mowinckel, Sigmund, *The Psalms in Israel's Worship*. Nashville: Abingdon Press, 1962.

Murphy, Roland, *Wisdom Literature & Psalms*. Nashville: Abingdon Press, 1983.

Ringgren, Helmer, *The Faith of the Psalmists*. Philadelphia: Fortress Press, 1963.

Sabourin, Leopold, *The Psalms: Their Origin and Meaning*. Staten Island, New York: Alba House, 1974.

Stuhlmueller, Carroll, *Psalms I*. Wilmington, Del.: Michael Glazier, Inc., 1983.

——————, *Psalms II*. Wilmington, Del.: Michael Glazier, Inc., 1983.

——————, "The Psalms and the Liturgy: The Heart and Heartbeat of Biblical Life" *The Bible Today* (March 1965) 1117-1125.

Terrien, Samuel, *The Psalms and Their Meaning for Today*. Indianapolis: Bobbs-Merrill, Inc., 1952.

Weiser, Artur, *Psalms: A Commentary*. Philadelphia: Westminster Press, 1962.

Westermann, Claus, *Praise and Lament in the Psalms*. Atlanta: John Knox Press, 1981.

Worden, Thomas W., *The Psalms Are Christian Prayer*. New York: Sheed & Ward, 1961.

Zerr, Bonaventure, *The Psalms: A New Translation*. Ramsey, N.J.: Paulist Press, 1979.